new testament

big picture/little picture
STUDY GUIDE

by Cali Black
creator of Come Follow Me Study

Created by Cali Black, Come Follow Me Study, LLC. This material is copyrighted. It is intended for use in one household. For additional permissions, contact Cali at comefollowmestudy@gmail.com.

This material is neither made, provided, approved, nor endorsed by Intellectual Reserve, Inc. or The Church of Jesus Christ of Latter-day Saints. Any content or opinions expressed, implied or included in or with the material are solely those of the owner and not those of Intellectual Reserve, Inc. or The Church of Jesus Christ of Latter-day Saints.

what to expect

Hey! I am SO glad that you are here.

I love the scriptures, and I love feeling confident while I read. Which meant that when I used to try to "study the scriptures", but I felt confused all the time, I didn't really have a great experience. I felt like everyone else "got it", and I was stuck with a kid-level understanding.

I've spent years trying to learn about the background info for all of these intricate scripture stories. I've learned about people, symbolism, cultural differences, and facts galore.

But I also know that most people don't have time to read elaborate and detailed historical books in order to learn all of this for yourselves.

So I started creating study guides that were for people like me. Latter-day Saints who:
- **wanted to feel like they understand the scriptures more**
- **but didn't have much extra time to devote to figuring it out**

As a former middle school teacher, I like to think I've mastered the art of simplification. I've taken countless hours of research and distilled them into what you REALLY need to know.

And then I realized that even more important than actually understanding what's going on in the scriptures, is figuring out how to apply them to my life and have them help to change me each day that I open their pages.

And thus, my Big Picture/Little Picture Study Guides were born.

The perfect mix of content, short summaries, a little bit of history, and a whole bunch of spiritual focus. I think it's a pretty good recipe.

If you've never used a Big Picture/Little Picture Study Guide, here's what to expect:

Each week, I give you EVERYTHING that you need to be successful on both ends of the scripture study spectrum: the background knowledge AND the spiritual application.

BIG PICTURE

In the Big Picture section, I give you whatever historical, contextual, or interesting knowledge I think that you'll need to totally "get" what's going on. (In simple, bullet-point form, of course.)

LITTLE PICTURE

After all that big context, we get to the nitty-gritty daily reading part.

I give a quick little reference for every single chapter that we read, including a couple of sentences about what you should know/remember BEFORE you read, and then a simple summary of WHAT you are reading in that chapter. (Just in case things get confusing!)

SPIRITUAL GUIDING QUESTIONS

This is, of course, where the rubber meets the road in WHY we study the scriptures. I've created 7 questions for you to ponder on each week, so you could respond to one each day, do them all at once, or pick and choose which questions resonate with you.

Pretty much, I've packed as much info into this little study guide as I could while still keeping a conversational feel, because talking about the scriptures is super fun.

If you've been wanting to feel "in the know" before Sunday School lessons, if you've been looking for an easier way to understand the scriptures in order to teach your kids, if you've been looking to boost your knowledge before YOU stand up and teach seminary, then I believe this study guide is exactly what you need.

Above all though, never let this study guide, or anything else for that matter, separate you from getting in the actual scriptures. In fact, I hope this guide encourages you to get in the scriptures more often. Nothing is more important than you, with the Spirit, reading the word of God!

I am so excited to share what I've learned about this section of the New Testament with you. These epistles and even John's Revelation can teach us so much about our Savior Jesus Christ.

For ease, this study guide has been broken into quarters for the year. The previous editions of January-March, April-June, and July-September are available on Amazon or through comefollowmestudy.com in case you missed them.

I love connecting with people and talking about the scriptures, so make sure you follow me on Instagram @comefollowmestudy, on Facebook.com/comefollowmestudy, or join my email list at comefollowmestudy.com. I also co-host the One Minute Scripture Study podcast wherever you listen to podcasts!

Alright, are you feeling ready?! Let's go! Happy Studying!

- Cali Black

cool features

General Context: These bullet points remind your brain what we studied the week before, and give you any context you need for the current reading.

Spiritual Themes: New for my New Testament study guides this year, I really felt that I wanted to give you a quick glance into what spiritual themes you'll find in the reading. These would be great to highlight or note in your scriptures as you actually study, or you can just keep them in mind and ponder as you read through the assigned chapters!

People to Know: This is a quick bullet point list that includes descriptions and extra info about any person (or GROUP of people, like Pharisees or publicans). Anyone that is mentioned in that week's reading gets put in the list so that you always have an easy reference!

Map: I can barely contain my excitement for this one. WE HAVE MAPS! I have to thank the fabulous Sarah Cook from Olivet Designs for creating maps that not only look good, but also give you tons of information. Every single week, you'll find a new custom map that shows all the locations and/or travel covered in that reading. And because they are unique for each week, you won't get bogged down in too many locations-- it's just what you need, and nothing more!

Spiritual Guiding Questions: This is where you get to put your own pencil to the paper and practice applying the scriptures. There are seven questions for each week, so you could ponder one each day, do them all at one time, or only focus on the questions that resonate with you. These also make great discussion questions for your family, or if you are a teacher!

SEPTEMBER 25 - OCTOBER 1

GALATIANS 1-6

"Walk in the Spirit"

BIG PICTURE

How to feel confident fitting in this week's readings with the entire New Testament

General Context:

- **Let's do a quick refresh of where we are in the New Testament at this point.** The New Testament can easily be split into 4 sections: the four Gospels, the acts of the apostles, the epistles, and revelation of the future. We are currently reading the epistles, which are letters that Paul and other church leaders wrote. But to make things a little tricky, the epistles are NOT organized chronologically! They are instead organized in length order, and they are grouped together by whether they were written by Paul to a church, written by Paul to an individual, or written by someone other than Paul. Ever since we read Romans, we've been working through Paul's epistles to churches. And that brings us to his letter to the Galatians!

- **Who were the Galatians?** Galatia was actually a large region with lots of different cities in it, including Antioch, Iconium, Lystra, and Derbe. Paul visited many of these cities on his first, second, and third missionary journeys. So when we talk about "Paul's Epistle to the Galatians", unfortunately, we can't get much more specific than that. Which city of saints Paul was actually addressing has never been identified! It is important to note that the Galatians would have been mostly Gentile converts to Christianity.

- **What was going on when Paul wrote this epistle?** Picture Paul in the middle of his third missionary journey. It is around A.D. 56. Paul had recently written his 2 epistles to the Corinthians, and would write to the Romans soon after this. He was traveling through Macedonia, and he had been serving a mission for the better part of the previous 10 years at this point.

- **Why did the Galatians get a letter?** Oh, these Galatians most certainly needed a letter from Paul! After being amongst these saints, testifying of Jesus, and pointing them away from the rigidness of "the law" years prior to this, Paul got word that the saints in Galatia had made a distinct and determined turn toward strict obedience of the Law of Moses. They even claimed to reject Paul's authority as an apostle. Since these saints were not originally Jewish but instead Gentile, this meant a complete transformation of their lifestyle, including eating customs, calendars, and of course, circumcision for men. The letter that Paul writes to the Galatians is commonly known as one of his most harsh epistles, underscored by both the severity of the Galatians errors and Paul's personal ties to these saints. Look for Paul trying to teach about his own apostleship, the importance of faith in Jesus Christ, and the dangers of clinging to outward actions as signs of religion.

Spiritual Themes:

Look for these themes as you read the chapters this week! Find examples in the scriptures, and ponder on what these themes can look like in your life.

- **Bondage vs. Freedom**

- **Fruits of the Spirit**

- **Salvation through Faith in Jesus Christ**

People to Know:

- **Paul**
    - Paul (also known by his Hebrew name Saul) was a devout Jew and Pharisee. He also was a Roman citizen by birth. He persecuted the new Christian believers after Jesus' resurrection and ascension and was a strict believer in the Law of Moses. On his way to arrest more Christian believers, Paul was stopped on the road to Damascus and saw a vision of Jesus Christ. Paul was converted to Christianity and became a powerful missionary, spreading the gospel to many Gentiles. Paul served three big missionary trips that are recorded in the book of Acts (and possibly a fourth one later). This week, we read Paul's letter to the saints in Galatia. Paul wrote this letter during his third mission, prior to being arrested in Jerusalem.
- **Peter**
    - Peter was the zealous and eager disciple of Jesus Christ who became a confident leader of the new Christian church. Headquartered in Jerusalem, Peter had visions and councils that inspired him to be a champion of accepting all Gentiles into the Christian church and setting aside the strict adherence to the Law of Moses.
- **Titus**
    - Titus was a Gentile who had been converted by Paul. He attended the "Jerusalem Council" where it was decided that Gentile converts did not need to be circumcised or follow all of the Law of Moses. He became a close and trusted friend to Paul. During Paul's third mission, Titus met up with Paul in Philippi, a city in Macedonia, and reported on the saints in Corinth.

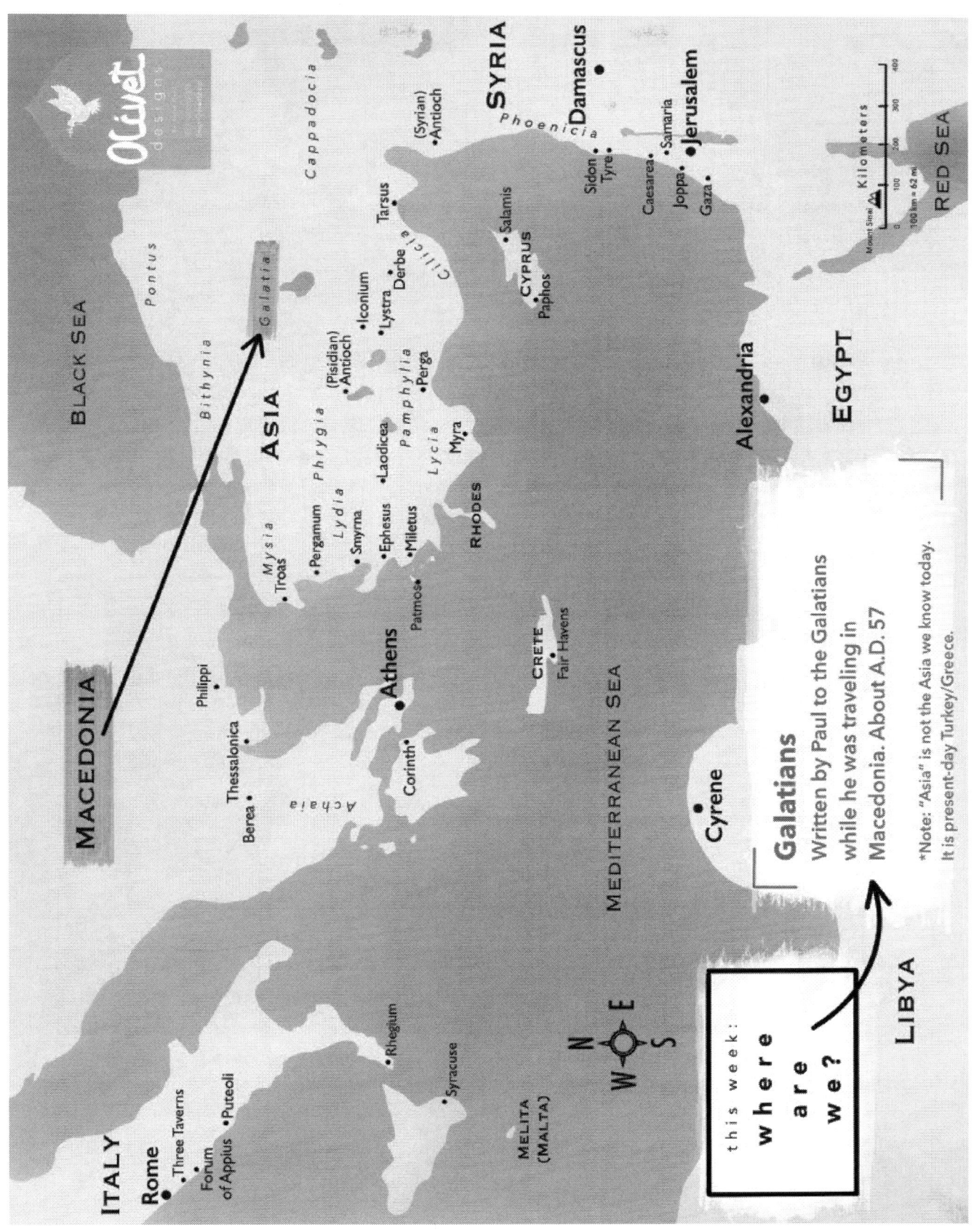

LITTLE PICTURE
How to understand each chapter and apply principles to my life

- **Galatians 1:**
    - **Before You Read:** This epistle was written by Paul as he traveled through Macedonia. He had recently visited some of the saints in Galatia, and then heard they had decided to completely turn to the Law of Moses. He doesn't directly address this issue in this first chapter, but he's setting the tone to explain why faith in Christ is what ultimately saves us.
    - **What You'll Read About:** Paul introduces himself as an apostle and warns against false gospels and teachers. He says true servants of Christ do not seek to please men, but to teach by revelation. He tells his conversion story of going from persecuting saints to seeing Christ and meeting with the apostles. He now travels and preaches to the Gentiles in various cities.

- **Galatians 2:**
    - **Before You Read:** In the previous chapter, Paul wrote about his conversion story all the way up to his current travels preaching the gospel to Gentiles in various cities.
    - **What You'll Read About:** Paul tells about a trip he took to Jerusalem with Barnabas and Titus 14 years after his conversion. He emphasizes that Titus, an uncircumcised Gentile, was accepted by the leadership in Jerusalem. Peter trusted Paul with the special responsibility to take the gospel to the Gentiles. Paul teaches that faith in Jesus Christ brings salvation, not the works of the Law of Moses.

- **Galatians 3:**
    - **Before You Read:** Paul has been writing to the Galatians to emphasize that Jesus Christ saves us, and not the Law of Moses. Don't miss the JST in the Appendix.
    - **What You'll Read About:** Paul asks the Galatians if they have received God's Spirit by faith, or by the law. He teaches that those with faith are the children of Abraham and inherit the Abrahamic Covenant. Relying on the law makes us cursed, but relying on Christ can adopt even Gentiles into the Abrahamic Covenant. The law acted as a teacher to point us to Christ who will actually justify us. When we are baptized, we become one in Christ.

- **Galatians 4:**
  - **Before You Read:** In the previous chapter, Paul wrote that faith in Christ is the way to salvation, not the law. He taught that we become the children of Christ and of Abraham through baptism and faith in Christ.
  - **What You'll Read About:** Paul compares a servant to a child, and explains that saints can become children and heirs of God through Christ. Paul calls the Galatians to repentance because they decided to return to the Law of Moses. He compares Abraham's two sons born of Agar (also known as Hagar, who was a servant in bondage) and Sarah (who was a free woman) to Mount Sinai (which represents the bondage of the Law of Moses) and Jerusalem (which represents the freedom from Christ). He says they are the children of promise, just like Isaac.

- **Galatians 5:**
  - **Before You Read:** In the previous chapter, Paul gave an allegory of Abraham and his two sons to show that we are free through following Christ, not the laws that came from Mount Sinai. The Galatians had decided to return to the Law of Moses and Paul is trying to correct them.
  - **What You'll Read About:** Paul instructs the saints to stand fast in Christ's freedom, because He makes us free, not the law. He teaches that the most important thing is not the law, but that we love our neighbor. He shows the importance of walking in the Spirit and not giving in to the desires of the flesh. Paul lists fruits of the Spirit, including love, joy, gentleness, and meekness.

- **Galatians 6:**
  - **Before You Read:** In the last chapter, Paul listed the fruits of the Spirit to show that we must walk in the Spirit and love our neighbor. Paul had a scribe write most of this epistle as he dictated it, but it was common for the author to actually write a few lines at the end of the epistle in their own handwriting. Paul takes over in verse 11, writing an unusually long postscript in his own hand.
  - **What You'll Read About:** Paul instructs the Galatians to bear one another's burdens. He teaches that we reap what we sow, whether it be things of the flesh or the Spirit. Don't be weary in well-doing. Paul ends his epistle by reiterating that salvation comes through Jesus Christ, not through the law.

SPIRITUAL GUIDING QUESTIONS

Question: When was a time in your life when you focused on pleasing other people more than pleasing God? What did you learn from this experience? (Galatians 1:10)

Question: What is one commandment or gospel principle that you used to just "go through the motions"? How has adding faith matured your understanding of that principle? (Galatians 2:16)

Question: How does faith play a role in feeling the Spirit? (Galatians 3:2)

Question: When has obedience to a commandment grown your faith in Jesus Christ? (Galatians 3:24)

Question: How has your faith in Jesus Christ brought more freedom into your life? (Galatians 5:1)

Question: What fruit of the gospel have you experienced recently? Which fruit would you like to seek after more? (Galatians 5:22)

Question: When has Jesus helped you feel less weary in your efforts to serve and do good? (Galatians 6:9)

OCTOBER 2 - OCTOBER 8

EPHESIANS 1-6

"For the Perfecting of the Saints"

BIG PICTURE

How to feel confident fitting in this week's readings with the entire New Testament

General Context:

- **We now move forward about 5 years!** Paul has written his epistles to the Corinthians, Galatians, and Romans, and completed his third missionary journey. He travels to Jerusalem where he ends up getting arrested, later being transferred to Caesarea, and then getting shipwrecked on his prisoner transport to Rome. (Review Acts 22-28 if you want a refresher on these events!) So basically, Paul had been imprisoned for a while since he wrote the epistles we just studied. He eventually made it to Rome, which is where the Book of Acts ends, but he was kept under house arrest. It is around this time, likely A.D. 60-62, that Paul writes a different group of epistles: Philippians, Colossians, Ephesians, Philemon, and Hebrews. This week, we will study Paul's epistle to the Ephesians!

- **Did Paul know the saints in Ephesus?** Paul had been to Ephesus quite a bit. He first visited the saints there at the end of his second missionary journey. Ephesus then became a huge missionary base during Paul's third journey, and he stayed for over two years (this is when he wrote 1 Corinthians). He eventually left Ephesus because of a big riot (read Acts 19 for a refresher). After spending multiple years of his life in Ephesus, Paul knew these saints well!

- **What is this epistle about?** This epistle has a generally positive tone! Paul is teaching what the Church of Christ should look like. He's sharing lots of important doctrines about Jesus. He also encourages unity by asking the saints to embrace their own individual spiritual gifts.

Spiritual Themes:

Look for these themes as you read the chapters this week! Find examples in the scriptures, and ponder on what these themes can look like in your life.

- **Unity**

- **The Love of Jesus**

- **Kindness**

People to Know:

- **Paul**
    - Paul (also known by his Hebrew name Saul) was a devout Jew and Pharisee. He was also a Roman citizen by birth. He persecuted the new Christian believers after Jesus' resurrection and ascension and was a strict believer in the Law of Moses. On his way to arrest more Christian believers, Paul was stopped on the road to Damascus and saw a vision of Jesus Christ. Paul was converted to Christianity and became a powerful missionary, spreading the gospel to many Gentiles. Paul served three big missionary trips that are recorded in the book of Acts (and possibly a fourth one later). This week, we read Paul's letter to the saints in Ephesus. Paul wrote this letter after his third mission and after a few years of imprisonment in Rome.
- **Tychicus**
    - Tychicus had been one of Paul's missionary companions at the end of his third missionary journey. He is the one who, now that Paul had made it to Rome under house arrest, was delivering some of the epistles that Paul wrote. Tychicus delivered the epistle to the Ephesians and the Colossians. He also accompanied Onesimus, the former slave who was returning to Philemon, referenced in the epistle to Philemon.

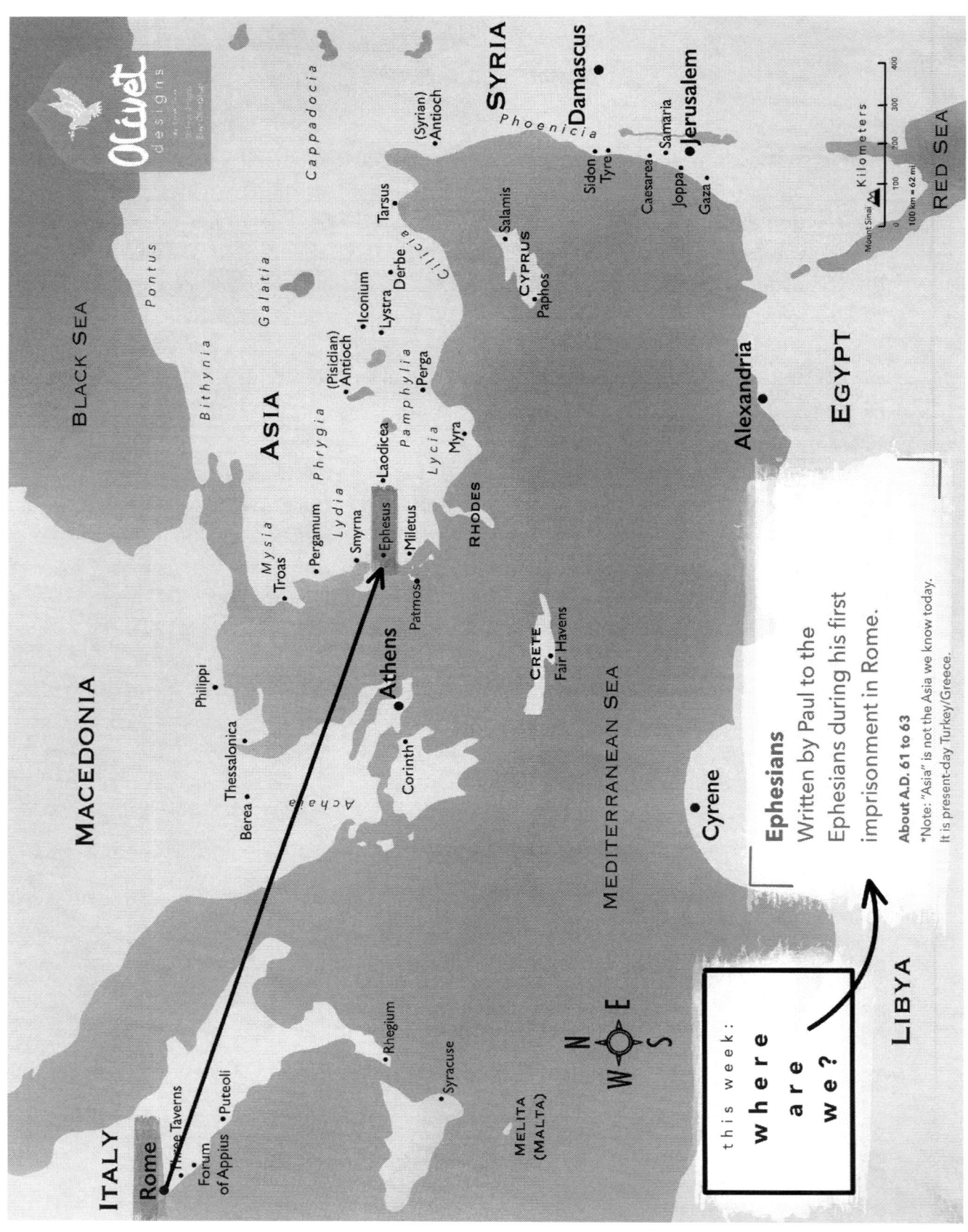

LITTLE PICTURE
How to understand each chapter and apply principles to my life

- **Ephesians 1:**
  - **Before You Read:** This chapter begins Paul's epistle to the Ephesians, which he wrote from Rome around A.D. 61-62. Paul had heard positive things about the faith and goodness of the saints in Ephesus, so look for what he chooses to teach them to extend their faith.
  - **What You'll Read About:** Paul greets the Ephesians, and teaches that God foreordained them to receive the gospel. He writes that we are redeemed through Christ's grace. God will gather together those belonging to Christ in the restoration. Through faith, saints are given the Spirit as a promise of salvation to come. Paul praises God's power and glory, and teaches that God will give the saints understanding and wisdom.

- **Ephesians 2:**
  - **Before You Read:** In the previous chapter, Paul wrote about the blessings promised to to faithful saints, including the Spirit, wisdom, understanding, and redemption.
  - **What You'll Read About:** Paul writes that God will save us from spiritual and physical death through mercy and love. We are saved through our faith in Christ's grace, not through works. Christ saves all, Jew and Gentile, and makes us one in Him. The church is built on prophets and apostles, with Christ as the cornerstone.

- **Ephesians 3:**
  - **Before You Read:** Paul has been writing to the Ephesians about the importance of unity in the church, and taught that the church is built on Jesus Christ. Remember that Paul is under house arrest in Rome at this time, thus his reference to being a "prisoner".
  - **What You'll Read About:** Paul teaches about the mysteries that have been revealed through revelation that have never before been known. Gentiles will inherit the same blessings of the gospel as Jews. Paul glories in the grace given to him in his weakness, and prays that Christ will dwell in the hearts of the Ephesians and strengthen them. Christ's love is beyond all understanding.

- **Ephesians 4:**
  - **Before You Read:** In the previous chapter, Paul taught about grace, Christ's love, and the mysteries that have been revealed to believers.
  - **What You'll Read About:** Paul emphasizes the importance of unity in the church by declaring that there is only one faith and one baptism. Christ gives us grace. He also sends apostles, prophets, and teachers to help edify and teach the church. They help us stay grounded in truth, not tossed about with every bit of doctrine. He warns not to be like some other Gentiles who lack understanding and are past feeling. He teaches them to let sin and bitterness go, and to be kind and forgiving.

- **Ephesians 5:**
  - **Before You Read:** In the previous chapter, Paul wrote to the Ephesians about letting go of sins like lying, anger, stealing and bitterness and instead being united with other saints in tenderhearted forgiveness.
  - **What You'll Read About:** Paul teaches that Christ gave himself as an offering, so saints should not engage in sins such as fornication, foolish talking, or idolatry. Saints should walk in the light of the Lord, not in darkness. He counsels them to be wise, not to drink in excess, to sing hymns to the Lord, and give thanks always. He compares husbands and wives to Christ and the church, and teaches that husbands and wives must love one another and be joined together.

- **Ephesians 6:**
  - **Before You Read:** In the previous chapter, Paul taught about the importance of walking in light, and taught that a husband and wife should love one another.
  - **What You'll Read About:** Paul teaches that children should obey and honor their parents and fathers should nurture their children. He teaches that servants should obey their masters, and masters should remember that Christ is the true Master. Paul explains that we are fighting powers of darkness and wickedness, so we must put on the whole armor of God. Paul says that he is writing from prison, so Tychicus will come to the Ephesians to comfort and minister to them. He sends peace, love, faith, and grace.

SPIRITUAL GUIDING QUESTIONS

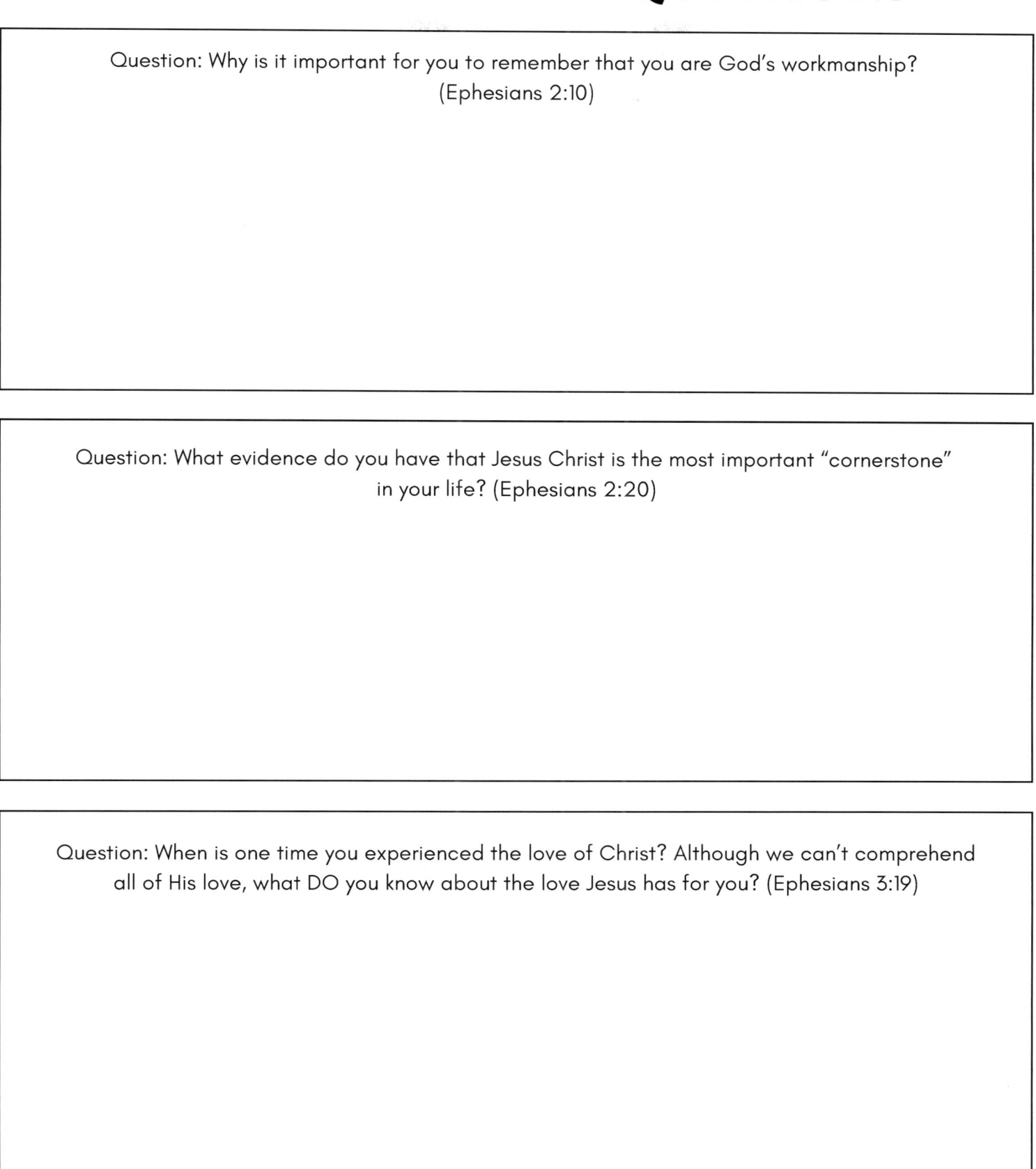

Question: Why is it important for you to remember that you are God's workmanship? (Ephesians 2:10)

Question: What evidence do you have that Jesus Christ is the most important "cornerstone" in your life? (Ephesians 2:20)

Question: When is one time you experienced the love of Christ? Although we can't comprehend all of His love, what DO you know about the love Jesus has for you? (Ephesians 3:19)

Question: How do you avoid having your testimony constantly tossed back and forth? What can you do when you feel your testimony starting to shake? (Ephesians 4:14)

Question: What is a kind thing you can do for someone today? What is a kind thing someone else has done for you recently? (Ephesians 4:32)

Question: When is a time that spiritual songs have helped you better worship the Lord? (Ephesians 5:19-20)

Question: Which part of the armor of God would you like to reinforce in your life? (Ephesians 6:13-18)

OCTOBER 9 - OCTOBER 15

PHILIPPIANS 1-4; COLOSSIANS 1-4

"I Can Do All Things through Christ Which Strengtheneth Me"

BIG PICTURE

How to feel confident fitting in this week's readings with the entire New Testament

General Context:

- **Ready to speed things up?** We've got TWO epistles to study this week. The nice thing is that they were both written around the same time. You'll remember that Paul served three missions, and then was arrested in Jerusalem. He spent a few years in prison, and was eventually transported (and shipwrecked!) to Rome. So now Paul is in Rome, still imprisoned in the form of house arrest. It's around A.D. 60-62, and Paul pens 5 epistles while imprisoned in Rome: **Philippians, Colossians, Ephesians (which we studied last week), Philemon, and Hebrews.**
- **Let's start with Philippians:** This epistle was the first that Paul wrote from prison in Rome. It is a letter focused on comforting and uplifting his fellow saints!
  - **What was Paul's relationship like with Philippi?** He had first visited Philippi on his second missionary trip. This city in Macedonia had tons of Romans and virtually no Jews. While Paul ended up being imprisoned there and having to invoke his Roman citizenship (read Acts 16 to brush up on this story!), the people that he helped convert to Christianity in Philippi became devoted saints. Paul passed through Philippi a few more times in future trips.
  - **So why an epistle?** This one actually has a sweet story. The saints in Philippi loved Paul so much that when they heard he was imprisoned in Rome, they sent a member from their town to help Paul. This man, Epaphroditus, traveled to Rome and attempted to help Paul, but when the work was too difficult, Epaphroditus returned to Philippi with this letter from Paul to help comfort and encourage the saints there.

- **Now let's talk about Colossians:** Paul's epistle to the Colossians was written right after his letter to the Philippians, still while he was imprisoned in Rome. It is a letter correcting the saints for errors in their worship and focusing them on Jesus Christ.
  - **What was Paul's relationship like with Colosse/Colossae?** It is actually possible that Paul had never visited Colosse prior to writing this epistle. That doesn't mean that the Colossians were all strangers, though- his friend Epaphras, and possibly even Timothy, first helped establish the church. The saints seemed to know who Paul was, and he had personal relationships with a few of them, especially some of the leaders.
  - **So why did he write them an epistle?** This epistle is also the result of a traveler. A man named Epaphras came from Colosse, bringing news to Paul of the mistakes the saints were making in his town. They had fallen into the trap of thinking external actions and strict rules would help them reach perfection. The saints believed that through their ceremonies and even angel worship, they could learn mysteries of the universe that no one else could. As you read, look for how Paul corrects the Colossians and points them toward Jesus as the source of salvation.
- **Something to keep in mind:** Paul also wrote his epistle to Philemon at around this same time, and Philemon lived in Colosse! So it's probable that both the epistles to the Colossians and to Philemon were delivered at the same time. We will study Philemon in a couple of weeks.

Spiritual Themes:

Look for these themes as you read the chapters this week! Find examples in the scriptures, and ponder on what these themes can look like in your life.

- **The Peace of God**

- **Qualities We Should Seek**

- **Jesus Christ is the Answer**

People to Know:

- **Paul**
  - Paul (also known by his Hebrew name Saul) was a devout Jew and Pharisee. He was also a Roman citizen by birth. He persecuted the new Christian believers after Jesus' resurrection and ascension and was a strict believer in the Law of Moses. On his way to arrest more Christian believers, Paul was stopped on the road to Damascus and saw a vision of Jesus Christ. Paul was converted to Christianity and became a powerful missionary, spreading the gospel to many Gentiles. Paul served three big missionary trips that are recorded in the book of Acts (and possibly a fourth one later). He ended up in house arrest in Rome, which is when he started to write a series of epistles, including these epistles to the Philippians and Colossians.
- **Timothy (Timotheus)**
  - Timothy was a disciple from Derbe. He became one of Paul's closest friends and accompanied him on many missionary travels. His mother was Jewish, but his father was Greek. He spent a lot of time in Corinth, and was with Paul when Paul wrote 2 Corinthians. Timothy was later present when Paul wrote both Philippians and Colossians.
- **Epaphroditus**
  - This man from Philippi was sent by the Philippians to assist Paul during his imprisonment in Rome. Epaphroditus arrived in Rome and helped Paul the best he could. Epaphroditus fell sick, but recovered, and Paul sent him back to Philippi with an epistle to the Philippians.
- **Epaphras**
  - Epaphras was a man from Colosse. He noticed the Colossian saints, while possessing many good qualities, were starting to focus on strict rules that outsiders had made in order to learn the mysteries of the universe. Epaphras traveled to Rome to find Paul as he was being held under house arrest. He told Paul of their situation in Colosse, and Paul penned the epistle to the Colossians in return.
- **Tychicus**
  - Tychicus had been one of Paul's missionary companions at the end of his third missionary journey. He is the one who, now that Paul had made it to Rome under house arrest, was delivering some of the epistles that Paul wrote. Tychicus delivered the epistles to the Ephesians and the Colossians. He was also accompanied by Onesimus, the former slave who was returning to Philemon, referenced in the epistle to Philemon.
- **Onesimus**
  - Onesimus was a former slave from Colosse who had robbed his master and fled to Rome. Once in Rome, he met Paul and was likely converted to Christianity. Paul wrote epistles to both the Colossians in general, and also to Philemon, who was Onesimus' former master. Onesimus and Tychicus traveled from Rome to Colosse with these two epistles.

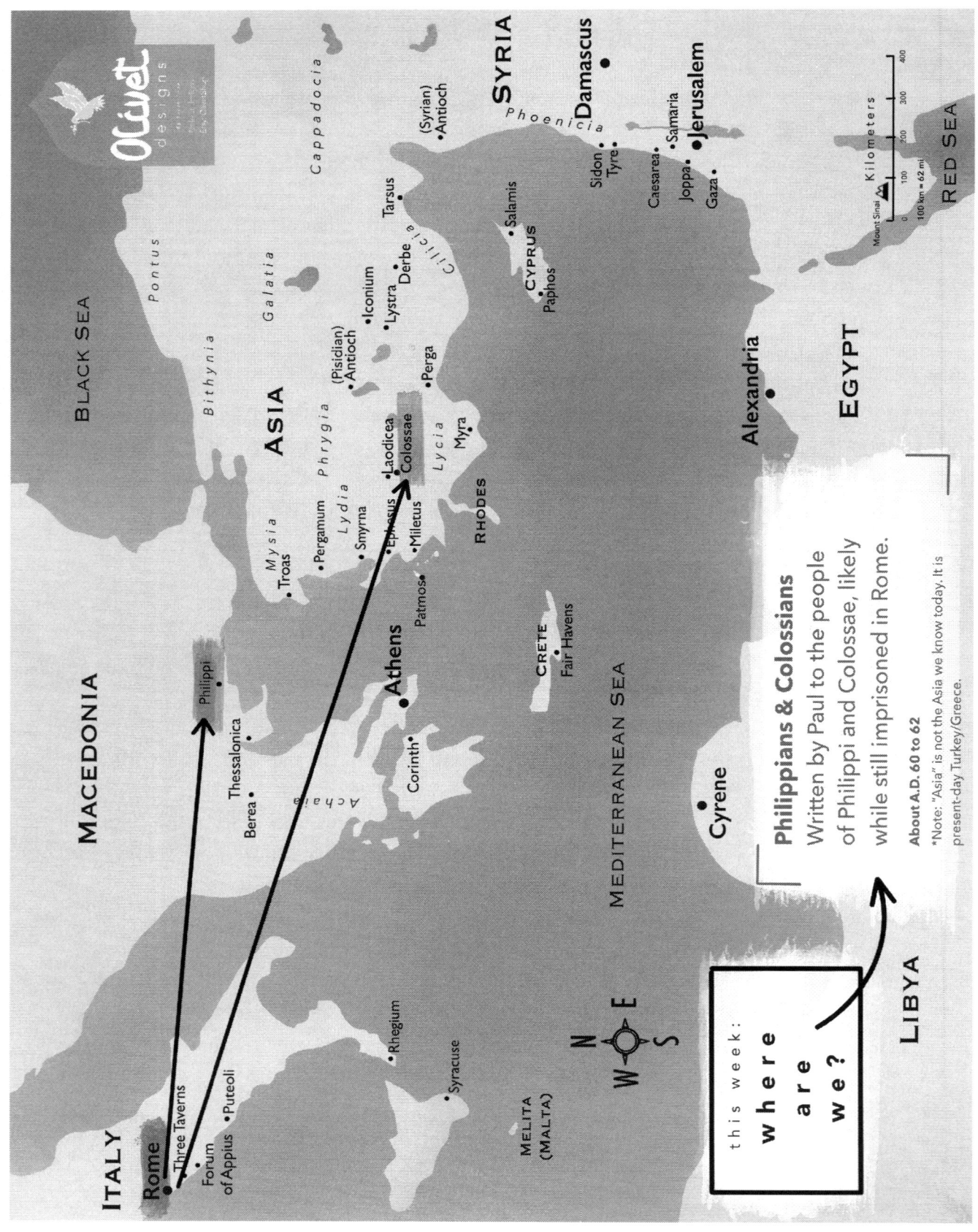

LITTLE PICTURE
How to understand each chapter and apply principles to my life

- **Philippians 1:**
  - **Before You Read:** Paul meant a lot to the saints in Philippi, and the Philippians meant a lot to Paul. You can feel that relationship in this chapter. Paul is writing from prison in Rome to hopefully comfort and strengthen the saints in Philippi.
  - **What You'll Read About:** Paul expresses gratitude for the goodness and fellowship of the Philippians, and prays for them that they will be filled with righteousness and sincerity. Paul assures the Philippians that the hardships he has endured have all worked for the advancement of the gospel because it has given others confidence to preach of Christ. He talks about living and continuing to preach, and of dying and being with Christ. He counsels the saints to be unified in the faith of the gospel.

- **Philippians 2:**
  - **Before You Read:** In the previous chapter, Paul wrote to the Philippians praising their faithfulness and counseling them to be unified.
  - **What You'll Read About:** Paul teaches that the saints should be of one mind, humble, and look after each other's things. When they do this, they follow Christ's example, who humbled Himself, was obedient, and died. Paul writes that they should be the sons of God through their obedience, and promises to send Timothy to look after the Philippians. He also mentions Epaphroditus, a Philippian who had gotten sick while ministering to Paul and who would now be returning to Philippi.

- **Philippians 3:**
  - **Before You Read:** Paul has been writing to the Philippians to teach about Christ's example of humility and obedience, and just finished explaining that Epaphroditus would be returning to them following a serious sickness.
  - **What You'll Read About:** Paul rejoices in Christ, and not in flesh. He describes his own background persecuting the church, but explains that he has lost everything in order to gain Christ. He presses forward toward Christ, forgetting what's behind. Paul teaches that saints must follow the right leaders who will lead them to Christ and the Resurrection.

- **Philippians 4:**
  - **Before You Read:** In the previous chapter, Paul wrote about pressing forward to follow Christ. In this chapter, he'll finish his letter to the Philippians. Look for JST in the footnotes.
  - **What You'll Read About:** Paul teaches to stand fast in the Lord, and gives some specific counsel to certain Philippian members. He teaches that if we do things with prayer and thanksgiving, the Lord will bless us with great peace. He lists certain good things we should think about, teaches us to be content in whatever circumstances we find ourselves, and that we can do all things through Christ. He acknowledges a gift the Philippians sent him, and ends his epistle.

- **Colossians 1:**
  - **Before You Read:** Paul had heard from Epaphras that the Colossians were focusing too much on strict observances as a way to be morally perfect and learn the mysteries of the universe. He is writing this epistle to refocus them on Christ as the author of their redemption and salvation.
  - **What You'll Read About:** Paul greets the saints in Colosse, praising their faith in Christ. He lists all the good things he prays that these saints might have, such as knowledge, wisdom, strength in Christ's glorious power, and an inheritance of light. He teaches that Christ delivered us from darkness and is the source of redemption and forgiveness. Christ is the Creator and in Him is a fulness of all things. Paul teaches that if the saints continue steadfastly in the faith, they will be saved and heavenly mysteries will be revealed.

- **Colossians 2:**
  - **Before You Read:** In the previous chapter, Paul praised the faith the Colossians have in Christ. He also focused on Christ as the Savior and Creator. Look for JST in the Appendix in this chapter.
  - **What You'll Read About:** Paul is sad not to be with the Colossians in person, but hopes that their hearts will be comforted through Christ, who is the source of wisdom and knowledge. He warns the saints of being deceived by the philosophies and traditions of men. Paul compares baptism to Christ's death and resurrection. He counsels the saints to focus on Christ, who is the Head, and not be distracted by meat, drink, angel worship, or vanity.

- **Colossians 3:**
  - **Before You Read:** In the previous chapter, Paul focuses on Christ as the source of wisdom and knowledge.
  - **What You'll Read About:** Paul teaches that if we are reborn with Christ, our lives become closer to God. He gives things to avoid, such as uncleanness, covetousness, anger, filthy communication, and lying. Instead, we must become a "new man" with kindness, meekness, forgiveness, and charity. He gives advice specific to wives, husbands, children, fathers, and servants. In the Lord, we will all receive our reward according to the good or bad we do.

- **Colossians 4:**
  - **Before You Read:** Paul has been writing about being reborn as a new man in Christ who is kind, forgiving, meek, and loving. In this chapter, Paul references an epistle he sent to the Laodiceans to request that the Colossians read that epistle as well. Unfortunately, that epistle has been lost, so don't go looking for the Epistle to the Laodiceans in your scriptures!
  - **What You'll Read About:** Paul teaches that the saints should continue in prayer and thanksgiving, and walk in wisdom. He counsels them to speak with grace. Paul lists some of the men who will come minister to the Colossians in his stead, including Tychicus and Onesimus. He instructs the Colossians to share this epistle with the Laodiceans, and for them to read his epistle to the Laodiceans (which we don't have), and closes his letter.

SPIRITUAL GUIDING QUESTIONS

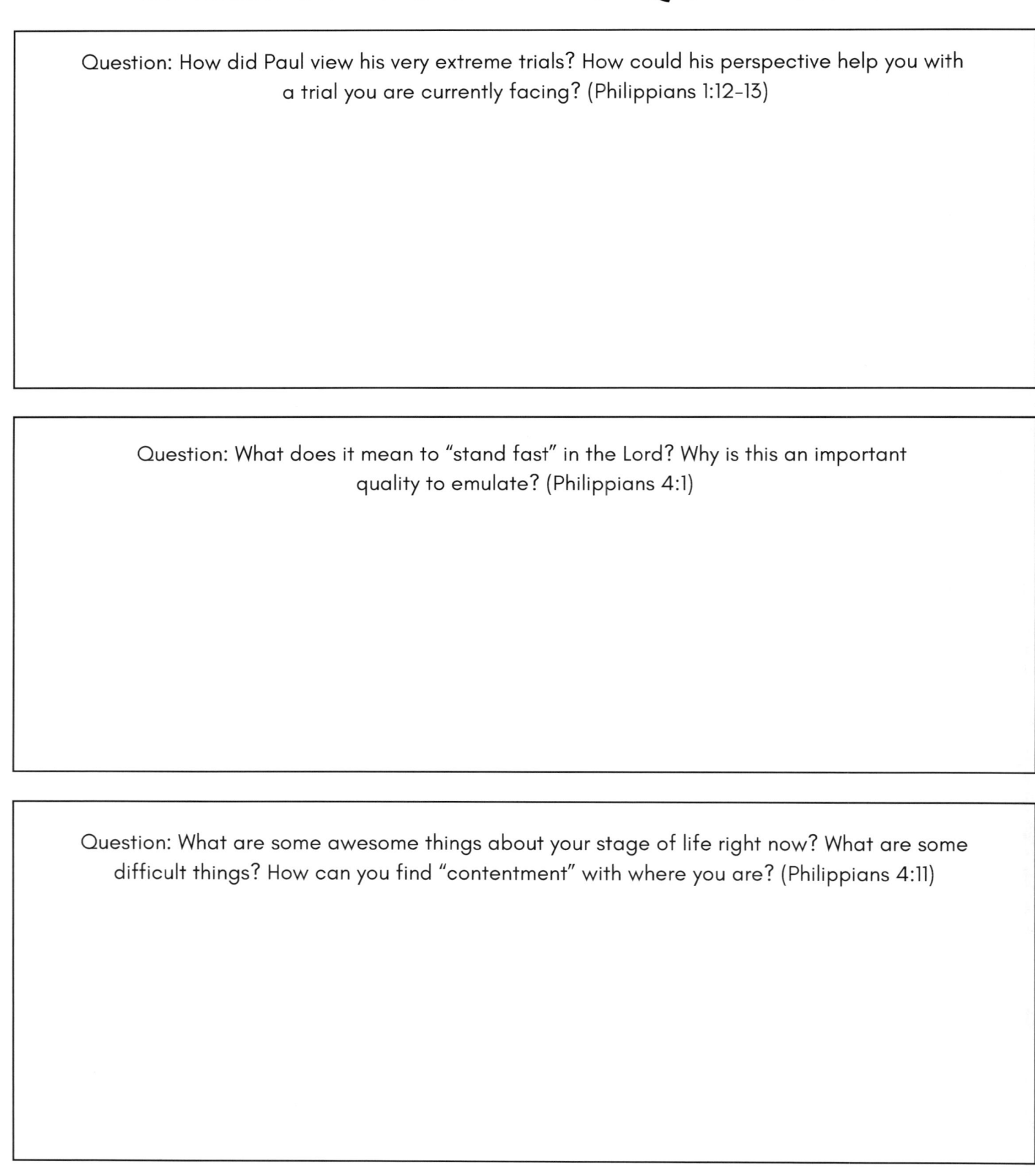

Question: How did Paul view his very extreme trials? How could his perspective help you with a trial you are currently facing? (Philippians 1:12-13)

Question: What does it mean to "stand fast" in the Lord? Why is this an important quality to emulate? (Philippians 4:1)

Question: What are some awesome things about your stage of life right now? What are some difficult things? How can you find "contentment" with where you are? (Philippians 4:11)

Question: How has Christ strengthened you? What do you think it means to do things "through Christ"? (Philippians 4:13)

Question: What does it look like to feel "grounded and settled" in your faith? How could you feel more firmly confident in your faith? (Colossians 1:23)

Question: How do you set your "affection" on heavenly things? Why is this important to you? (Colossians 3:2)

Question: Does peace "rule" in your heart right now? How could you allow Christ's peace to take over more of your heart? (Colossians 3:15)

OCTOBER 16 - OCTOBER 22

1 AND 2 THESSALONIANS

"Perfect That Which Is Lacking in Your Faith"

BIG PICTURE

How to feel confident fitting in this week's readings with the entire New Testament

General Context:

- **Let's start with a quick refresher of Paul's letters:** Paul wrote a lot of epistles, and while they can seem confusing to keep straight, they actually pretty easily fall into 4 clusters for when he wrote them:
  - **1 and 2 Thessalonians** were written in A.D. 50-51
  - **1 and 2 Corinthians, Galatians, and Romans** were written in A.D. 55-57 (we have studied all these already, and they were all during Paul's third missionary journey)
  - **Philippians, Colossians, Ephesians, Philemon, and Hebrews** were written in A.D. 60-62 (we've studied 3 of these, and they were all during Paul's house arrest imprisonment in Rome)
  - **Titus, 1 and 2 Timothy** were written in A.D. 64-65
- **This week, we are jumping backward about 10 years from where we were last week.** The years A.D. 50-51 were very early on in Paul's ministry, and the Jerusalem Council (where it was decided that Gentiles did not have to follow all of the Law of Moses) had just barely happened in A.D. 49.
- **The Epistles to the Thessalonians** would have been the first epistles if the New Testament had been organized chronologically. Paul first arrived in Thessalonica during his second missionary journey (Read Acts 17 if you want a refresher!). Paul was now in Corinth. Remember, this is BEFORE his epistles to the Corinthians, so this is when Paul was first establishing the church there in Corinth.
  - **The First Epistle to the Thessalonians** was sent because Paul's friend Timothy had visited Thessalonica. Timothy then returned to Paul in Corinth. Paul really wanted to go visit the saints in Thessalonica, but wasn't able to at this time, so he wrote an epistle and gave it to Timothy to deliver back to these saints.
  - **What was in this first epistle?** Paul wrote his letter as a result of what Timothy had reported to him about how these saints were doing. Since Timothy had told Paul that for the most part, the saints were living with faith and love for each other, Paul praised their goodness in much of his letter. He also heard that there was an unhealthy focus on ordinances and actions, so some of the epistle focuses on the importance of Christ as our Redeemer.

- ○ **The Second Epistle to the Thessalonians** came only about a year after the first one, and was mostly written to correct and clarify.
- ○ **What was the second letter about?** In Paul's first epistle, he had taught about Christ's Second Coming, teaching that it would come like a "thief in the night". This apparently led some to the incorrect belief that Christ would come immediately. In this second shorter epistle, Paul corrects this misunderstanding, shows gratitude for their faithfulness, and shows support for the saints despite the persecution they had been facing.
- **The authors for both epistles to the Thessalonians** are listed as Paul, Silas (Silvanus), and Timothy (Timotheus).

Spiritual Themes:

Look for these themes as you read the chapters this week! Find examples in the scriptures, and ponder on what these themes can look like in your life.

- **Prayer**

- **Loving One Another**

- **The Second Coming of Jesus Christ**

People to Know:

- **Paul**
  - ○ Paul (also known by his Hebrew name Saul) was a devout Jew and Pharisee. He was also a Roman citizen by birth. He persecuted the new Christian believers after Jesus' resurrection and ascension and was a strict believer in the Law of Moses. On his way to arrest more Christian believers, Paul was stopped on the road to Damascus and saw a vision of Jesus Christ. Paul was converted to Christianity and became a powerful missionary, spreading the gospel to many Gentiles. Paul served three big missionary trips that are recorded in the book of Acts (and possibly a fourth one later). This week, we read Paul's letter to the saints in Thessalonica, which he wrote during his second missionary trip.

- **Timothy (Timotheus)**
  - Timothy was a disciple from Derbe. He became one of Paul's closest friends and accompanied him on many missionary travels. His mother was Jewish, but his father was Greek. During Paul's second missionary trip, Timothy traveled to Thessalonica a few times on Paul's behalf, delivering reports to Paul and epistles to the Thessalonians. Timothy would later spend a lot of time in Corinth, and was with Paul when Paul wrote 2 Corinthians. Timothy was later present when Paul wrote both Philippians and Colossians.
- **Silas (Silvanus)**
  - Silas was one of the church leaders in Jerusalem who was sent to Antioch with Judas, Paul, and Barnabas with the official word that new Gentile converts did not need to fully follow the Law of Moses. Silas then became Paul's new missionary companion, and they departed on Paul's second mission together. It was during this second mission that Paul penned the two epistles to the Thessalonians, with Silas' assistance.

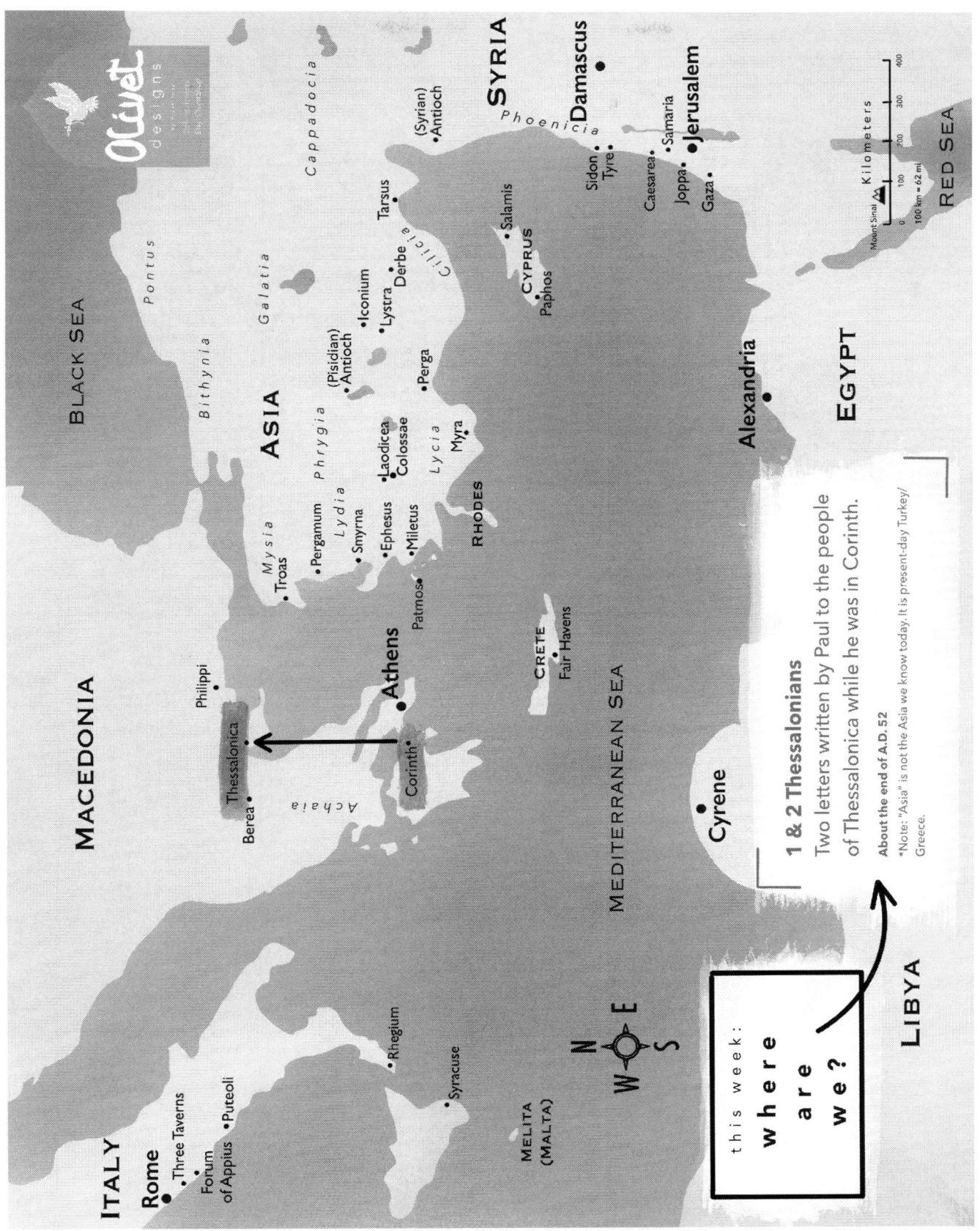

LITTLE PICTURE
How to understand each chapter and apply principles to my life

- **1 Thessalonians 1:**
  - **Before You Read:** Paul wrote this epistle around A.D. 50, back before he was imprisoned in Rome. He had hoped to visit the Thessalonians himself, but wrote this epistle after Timothy returned from a visit to Thessalonica.
  - **What You'll Read About:** Paul writes with gratitude for the faith, love, and patience of the saints in Thessalonica. He writes that the Thessalonians had been examples and missionaries to others in Macedonia and Achaia and praises their faith in Jesus.

- **1 Thessalonians 2:**
  - **Before You Read:** In the previous chapter, Paul greeted the Thessalonians and praised their faith and example to others around them.
  - **What You'll Read About:** Paul teaches that he and other true ministers of God teach and exhort not in deceit, flattery, or to please men, but to please God. He reminds them that they should always work hard to avoid becoming a burden. He praises the saints for their faith and steadfastness even in suffering. He says they are his glory and joy.

- **1 Thessalonians 3:**
  - **Before You Read:** In the previous chapter, Paul wrote with gratitude to the Thessalonians for their goodness, and pointed out the ways he and his fellow missionaries looked to please God, and not men. Remember that at this point, Paul is writing from Corinth, and Timothy just returned from a trip to Thessalonica because Paul had not been able to make the journey.
  - **What You'll Read About:** Paul writes about how he sent Timothy to visit Thessalonica when he could not. He describes how he rejoiced and was comforted when Timothy brought news of the faithfulness of the Thessalonians. He prays for the saints to perfect their faith and abound in love with each other.

- **1 Thessalonians 4:**
  - **Before You Read:** Paul just finished praising the Thessalonians for their goodness and faithfulness, and counseled them to perfect their faith. Look for JST in the footnotes.
  - **What You'll Read About:** Paul reminds the Thessalonians of some important commandments, including abstaining from fornication, and not defrauding or despising others. He praises the way they already love, and encourages them to love even more. Paul counsels them to work hard. He teaches that those who die in Christ will rise again and join with Him when He comes again.

- **1 Thessalonians 5:**
  - **Before You Read:** In the previous chapter, Paul wrote about how knowledge of the Resurrection and Second Coming can comfort saints. Look for JST in the footnotes.
  - **What You'll Read About:** Paul writes that Christ will come again like a thief in the night, but His followers have no need to fear. He teaches that we are the children of light, and that we must be sober and put on the armor of God. He gives more counsel to comfort and edify one another, be at peace, support the weak, and rejoice evermore. He teaches them to pray without ceasing, give thanks, and abstain from the appearance of evil. He prays for the saints and ends his epistle.

- **2 Thessalonians 1:**
  - **Before You Read:** This second epistle to the Thessalonians was written by Paul about a year after the first one. After the first epistle, the church had faced persecution and difficulty in Thessalonica, and the saints had been faithful. However, many misunderstood some of Paul's teachings on the Second Coming. He writes to both build up the saints, and to correct their misunderstanding in this chapter and the next. Look for JST in the footnotes.
  - **What You'll Read About:** Paul and his companions greet the Thessalonians and thank God for their growing faith and charity. Paul praises the way they have endured persecution. He writes that when Jesus comes again, the saints will be able to rest, and the wicked will be punished.

- **2 Thessalonians 2:**
  - **Before You Read:** In the previous chapter, Paul began to write about the Second Coming, and that Jesus will take vengeance on those who have not listened to Him. In this chapter, look for how Paul corrects the misunderstanding that the Second Coming will occur immediately. Be sure to check out the JST in the Appendix for verses 7-9 of this chapter, as well as other JST in the footnotes.
  - **What You'll Read About:** Paul clarifies that the Second Coming will not come until after there is a falling away (apostasy). Christ will allow Satan to work and have power, until Christ comes to judge the unrighteous. Paul counsels the saints to stand fast in the teachings they've received, and teaches that God has given us everlasting consolation.

- **2 Thessalonians 3:**
  - **Before You Read:** In the previous chapter, Paul wrote to clarify that before Christ comes again, there will be a great apostasy.
  - **What You'll Read About:** Paul asks for the saints' prayers on behalf of the missionaries. He commands them to remove anyone who acts disorderly, and that if someone does not work, he will not eat. He teaches them to quietly work hard for their food, and to not be weary in well doing. He sends peace and salutations and closes his letter.

SPIRITUAL GUIDING QUESTIONS

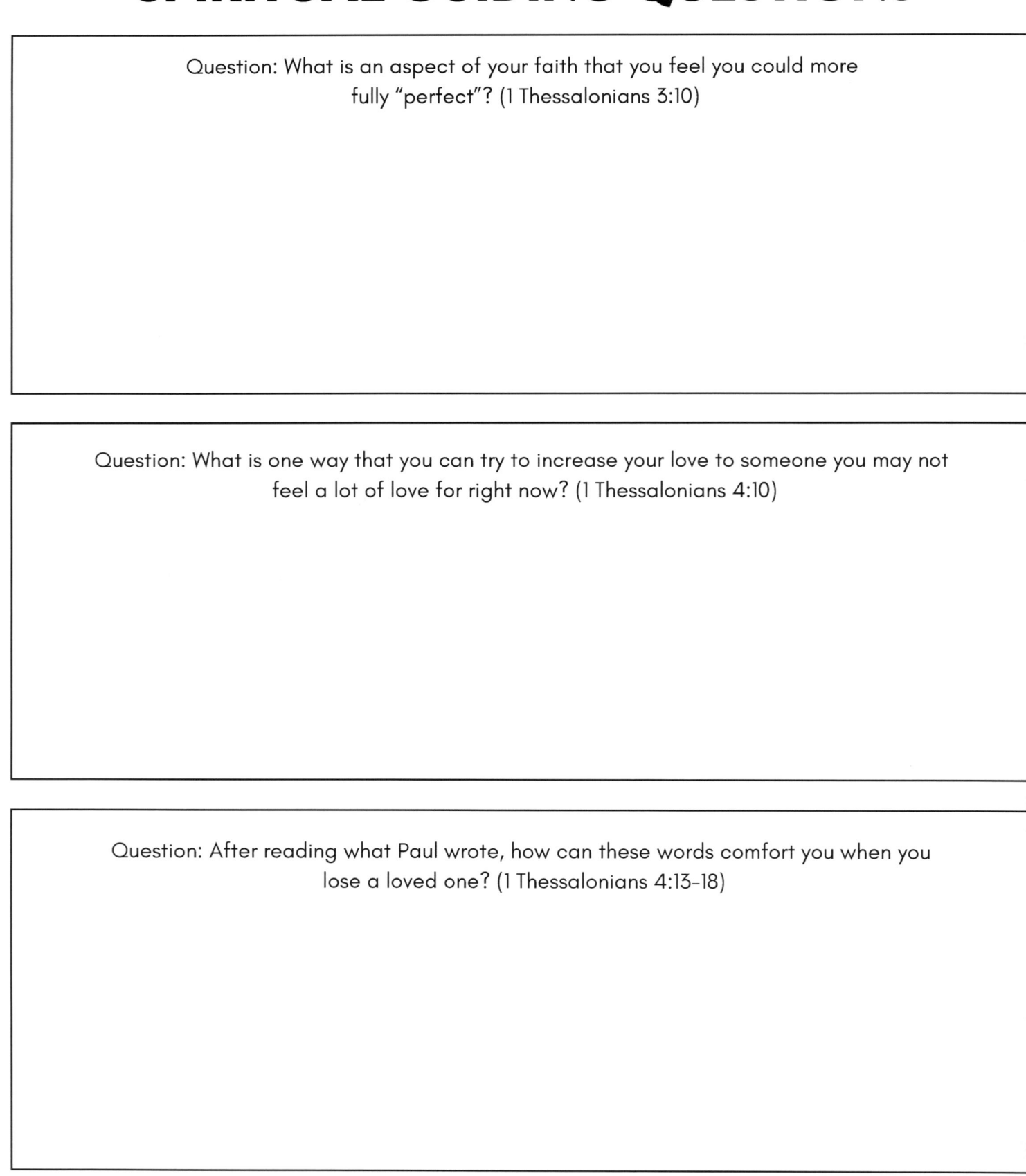

Question: What is an aspect of your faith that you feel you could more fully "perfect"? (1 Thessalonians 3:10)

Question: What is one way that you can try to increase your love to someone you may not feel a lot of love for right now? (1 Thessalonians 4:10)

Question: After reading what Paul wrote, how can these words comfort you when you lose a loved one? (1 Thessalonians 4:13-18)

Question: Which phrase from Paul's counsel stands out to you as a reminder you need in your life right now? (1 Thessalonians 5:14-22)

Question: When has exercising patience during a trial been a blessing? (2 Thessalonians 1:4)

Question: What is the difference between the "rest" the Lord offers and the "rest" the world talks about? (2 Thessalonians 1:7)

Question: Why does the Lord encourage us to be industrious instead of being idle? How could you add more meaningful work to your life? (2 Thessalonians 3:8-13)

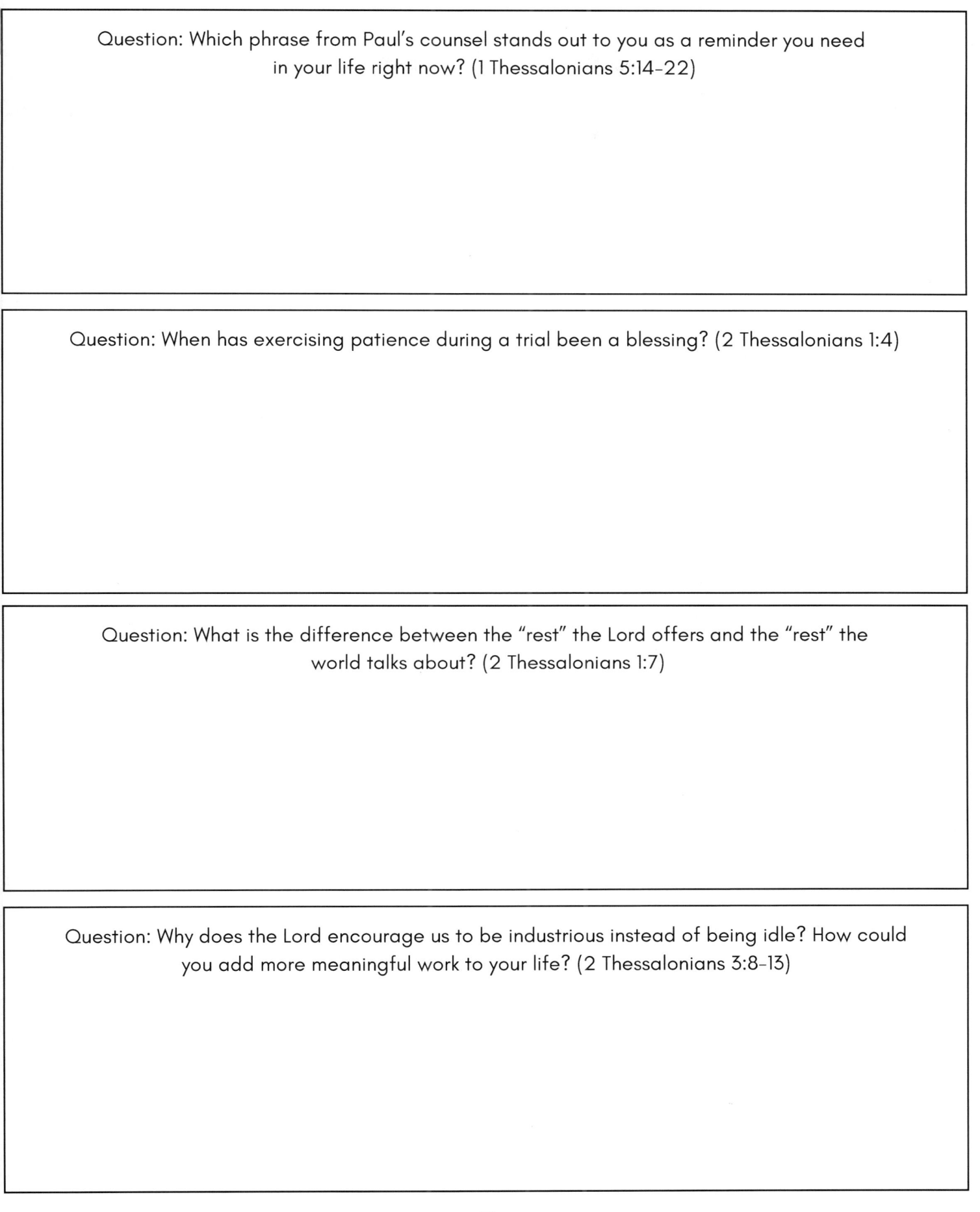

OCTOBER 23 - OCTOBER 29

1 AND 2 TIMOTHY; TITUS; PHILEMON

"Be Thou an Example of the Believers"

BIG PICTURE

How to feel confident fitting in this week's readings with the entire New Testament

General Context:

- **This week, we'll start by focusing on Paul's final three epistles.** These epistles are unique because they are written by Paul to individuals, not to groups or churches. Since these individuals, **Timothy and Titus**, were church leaders, you'll notice that the epistles focus more on church organization and discipline issues. They are often referred to as the "pastoral epistles" because they were both written to "pastors".
- **1 and 2 Timothy and Titus were written after the history in the Book of Acts ended.** You may remember that the Book of Acts left off when Paul was imprisoned in Rome. We've also already studied most of the grouping of epistles that Paul wrote during this imprisonment, including Ephesians, Philippians, and Colossians. But now we move forward a few years to around A.D. 64-65. Paul has been released from prison in Rome and has been going around to visit congregations and friends. Paul writes 1 Timothy and Titus during this period of freedom. Paul is then imprisoned again in Rome, and he writes his 2nd epistle to Timothy from prison. Shortly after he writes this letter, Paul is martyred in Rome.
  - **Who is Timothy?** Timothy, or Timotheus, was a man we met way back in Acts 16 who became one of Paul's most trusted companions and fellow missionaries. His dad was Greek and his mom was Jewish. Timothy was the one Paul sent to visit many cities such as Thessalonica, Macedonia, and Corinth when Paul himself could not. Timothy even helped Paul write many of the epistles!
  - **First Timothy** was written around A.D. 64, soon after Paul's release from being imprisoned in Rome. He had previously been with Timothy in Ephesus, and Paul left Timothy there to keep tabs on the congregation. Paul wrote this epistle, likely from somewhere in Macedonia, to encourage Timothy. He also gives him some counsel and teaches about Jesus.
  - **Second Timothy** is the final epistle Paul wrote shortly before his martyrdom, around A.D. 65. Note that chronologically, Titus (which we'll read next) actually comes between the two epistles to Timothy. At the time this letter was written, Paul was imprisoned in Rome, about to be brought before wicked Emperor Nero for the second time. In the epistle, we will see Paul's mindset as he shows great courage and trust in the Lord.

- ○ **And who is Titus?** Titus was one of Paul's companions and fellow church leaders. He was a Gentile who Paul had converted, and they had traveled to the Jerusalem Council together. He accompanied Paul on his third missionary journey, and he was also the one Paul sent to deliver both his epistles to the Corinthians.
- ○ **At the time of Paul's epistle to Titus,** Paul was experiencing freedom after being imprisoned in Rome (same time period as 1 Timothy). Titus and Paul were in Ephesus together, then traveled to Crete. Paul then continued on and sent Titus this letter to encourage him in his work.
- **And what about Philemon?** The epistle to Philemon is super unique! Philemon was written while Paul was first imprisoned in Rome between A.D. 60-62 (same time as Ephesians, Philippians, and Colossians). In fact, it was written at the exact same time as Paul's letter to the Colossians. You might remember that Paul sent the missionary Tychius to Colosse with their epistle, but Tychius was not alone! Tychius was accompanied by Onesimus, who was a runaway slave. Onesimus had belonged to Philemon in Colosse, but had robbed Philemon and ran away to Rome. Once in Rome, Onesimus met Paul and was presumably converted. Paul was now sending Onesimus back to Colosse with a letter to give to his former owner Philemon. This epistle encourages Philemon to accept Onesimus as a fellow Christian and to forgive him.

Spiritual Themes:

Look for these themes as you read the chapters this week! Find examples in the scriptures, and ponder on what these themes can look like in your life.

- **Being an Example**
- **Enduring to the End**
- **Forgiveness**

People to Know:

- **Paul**
  - Paul (also known by his Hebrew name Saul) was a devout Jew and Pharisee. He also was a Roman citizen by birth. He persecuted the new Christian believers after Jesus' resurrection and ascension and was a strict believer in the Law of Moses. On his way to arrest more Christian believers, Paul was stopped on the road to Damascus and saw a vision of Jesus Christ. Paul was converted to Christianity and became a powerful missionary, spreading the gospel to many Gentiles. Paul served three big missionary trips that are recorded in the book of Acts. He was then imprisoned in Rome, which is when he penned his epistle to Philemon. After being released, he traveled around again, presumably serving a fourth mission trip. This is when Paul wrote 1 Timothy and Titus. Paul was then imprisoned in Rome again, which is when he wrote 2 Timothy. Paul was martyred in Rome shortly after.
- **Timothy (Timotheus)**
  - Timothy was a disciple from Derbe. He became one of Paul's closest friends and accompanied him on many missionary travels. His mother was Jewish, but his father was Greek. During Paul's second missionary trip, Timothy traveled to Thessalonica a few times on Paul's behalf, delivering reports to Paul and epistles to the Thessalonians. Timothy would later spend a lot of time in Corinth, and was with Paul when Paul wrote 2 Corinthians. Timothy was later present when Paul wrote both Philippians and Colossians. Following Paul's imprisonment in Rome, Timothy traveled briefly with Paul. Paul wrote Timothy two epistles.
- **Titus**
  - Titus was a Gentile who had been converted by Paul. He attended the "Jerusalem Council" where it was decided that Gentile converts did not need to be circumcised or follow all of the Law of Moses. He became a close and trusted friend to Paul. During Paul's third mission, Titus met up with Paul in Philippi and reported on the saints in Corinth. Following Paul's imprisonment in Rome, Paul and Titus traveled together for a while before they separated. Paul then wrote Titus an epistle.
- **Onesimus**
  - Onesimus was a former slave from Colosse who had robbed his master and fled to Rome. Once in Rome, he met Paul and was likely converted to Christianity. Paul wrote epistles to both the Colossians in general, and also Philemon, who was Onesimus' former master. Onesimus and Tychicus traveled from Rome to Colosse with these two epistles.

- **Philemon**
    - Philemon was a man of great faith who lived in Colosse. He hosted church in his home, and Paul had previously visited with him. He owned at least one slave, as was common with many affluent people at the time. Philemon's slave Onesimus robbed him and ran away. Paul sent Onesimus back to Colosse with an epistle for his friend Philemon, encouraging him to accept Onesimus as a new disciple of Christ. Although we never get an actual resolution to this story, it seems clear from Paul's epistle that he fully expected his friend Philemon to follow through on his request.

1 & 2 Timothy, Titus & Philemon

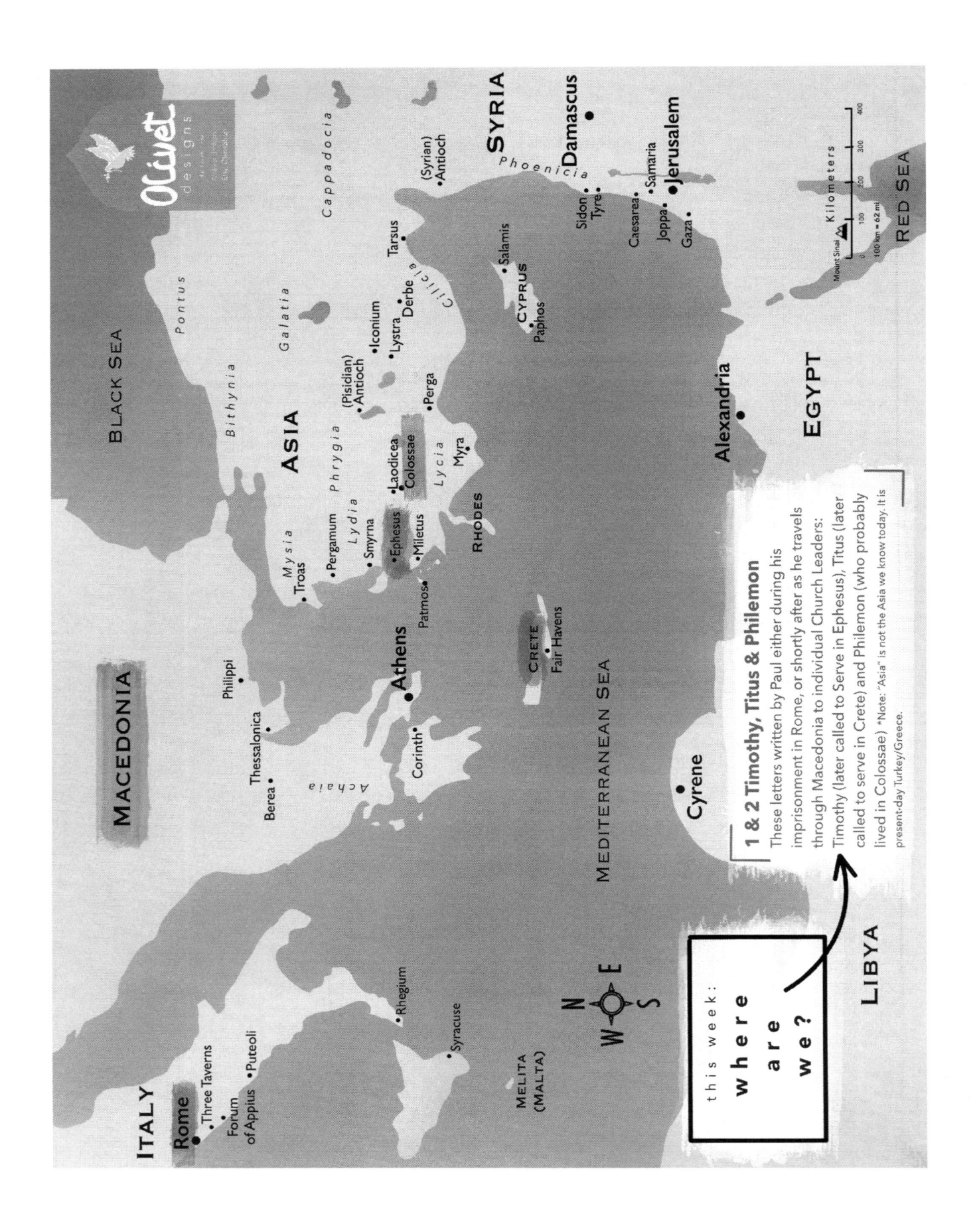

These letters written by Paul either during his imprisonment in Rome, or shortly after as he travels through Macedonia to individual Church Leaders: Timothy (later called to Serve in Ephesus), Titus (later called to serve in Crete) and Philemon (who probably lived in Colossae) *Note: "Asia" is not the Asia we know today. It is present-day Turkey/Greece.

this week: **where are we?**

LITTLE PICTURE
How to understand each chapter and apply principles to my life

- **1 Timothy 1:**
  - **Before You Read:** Paul is writing this epistle to his good friend, convert, and fellow missionary who he left in Ephesus while Paul continued to Macedonia. He is hoping to encourage, comfort, and teach Timothy. In this chapter, you'll notice Paul calls Timothy his son a couple of times. He's not actually his son! He means it spiritually – that Paul helped to convert and teach Timothy.
  - **What You'll Read About:** Paul greets Timothy and reminds him that the whole point of the commandments and the gospel is charity. He teaches that the law is made for the disobedient sinners. Paul gives thanks that Christ chose and enabled him, who was a persecutor and sinner. He testifies that Christ's grace is enough for all sinners.

- **1 Timothy 2:**
  - **Before You Read:** In the previous chapter, Paul wrote about the mercy and grace of Christ who can save even the worst of sinners. Remember that this epistle is a "Pastoral epistle", meaning it's written to a fellow church leader and will often discuss general church counsel even though it's written to just one man. Look for JST in the footnotes.
  - **What You'll Read About:** Paul counsels that we should pray for our leaders that we can live quiet and peaceful lives. Christ is our ransom and mediator. Paul gives a model for a godly woman, emphasizing modesty and charity.

- **1 Timothy 3:**
  - **Before You Read:** In the previous chapter, Paul taught that Christ is our mediator. Remember that Paul is giving organizational directions to Timothy, so it makes sense for him to list out the qualifications for various positions in the church. Note the JST in verses 15-16 of this chapter, which moves the phrase "The pillar and ground of the truth is" to verse 16.
  - **What You'll Read About:** Paul describes the qualifications for a bishop: blameless, vigilant, a teacher, patient, and a good leader in his own house. He lists similar qualifications for deacons, that they be honest, not drunk, pure of conscience, and lead their households well. He teaches truths about Christ, and that great is the mystery of godliness.

- **1 Timothy 4:**
  - **Before You Read:** In the previous chapter, Paul listed qualifications for bishops and deacons in the church.
  - **What You'll Read About:** Paul writes about apostasy in the latter-days, teaching that some will follow seducing spirits instead of true doctrine. Godliness is most important because it benefits us in this life and the next. He gives advice to Timothy to be an example of the believers, read doctrine, and to not neglect his priesthood.

- **1 Timothy 5:**
  - **Before You Read:** Paul has been writing to Timothy encouraging him to continue in the faith. Timothy is a leader and missionary in the church as well, so Paul focuses much of this chapter on the more administrative side of the church.
  - **What You'll Read About:** Paul teaches that we must treat elders with respect and to give support to widows in need. He teaches that even widows must work hard and do good works, not becoming idle. Paul gives policies concerning widows and elders, and teaches not to hastily call someone to be a leader.

- **1 Timothy 6:**
  - **Before You Read:** In the previous chapter, Paul wrote about the importance of caring for widows, and laid out policies for church elders. This is the final chapter in 1 Timothy. Look for JST in the Appendix.
  - **What You'll Read About:** Paul writes that servants should honor their master. Those who teach against Christ's words are proud and think that riches are godliness. We should be content with having food and raiment because the love of money is the root of all evil. Do not trust in riches, but trust in Christ, our ruler who gives us life. Paul encourages Timothy to keep pressing on and ends his epistle.

- **2 Timothy 1:**
  - **Before You Read:** Paul wrote this epistle to Timothy while he was imprisoned for the second time, and shortly before his martyrdom. Timothy was one of the people who had stuck by Paul's side through all his imprisonment and persecution. He is writing to Timothy to encourage him in the faith.
  - **What You'll Read About:** Paul greets Timothy and gives thanks for his goodness and faith. He teaches that God doesn't give us fear, and that we shouldn't be ashamed of our testimony. Paul lists some of the former friends who have turned on him in his imprisonment, and some who have remained faithful.

- **2 Timothy 2:**
  - **Before You Read:** In the previous chapter, Paul taught Timothy that God gives us the spirit of power and love, and listed some people who had turned on him and some who had stuck by his side.
  - **What You'll Read About:** Paul counsels Timothy to continue in the faith through difficulties. He teaches that his imprisonment and other trials do not stop the work of Christ, but our suffering means we can rise again with Christ. We must study the scriptures so we can plainly understand and teach truth. Paul teaches to avoid foolishness and youthful desires, but to follow faith, charity, and peace.

- **2 Timothy 3:**
  - **Before You Read:** Paul has been teaching Timothy about seeking out righteousness, faith, charity, and peace.
  - **What You'll Read About:** Paul describes how many will act in the last days, prioritizing their own pride and pleasure over God's will. Men will try to learn, but will never be able to get the whole truth. Those who live devoted to God will suffer persecution. All scripture is given through God's inspiration and can be used to perfect men.

- **2 Timothy 4:**
  - **Before You Read:** In the previous chapter, Paul described the way people will act during the coming apostasy. This chapter chronologically contains the final words we have from Paul before his martyrdom. Pay attention to his final teachings to his friend and companion Timothy. Look for JST in the footnotes.
  - **What You'll Read About:** Paul exhorts Timothy to be bold in preaching, reproving, and rebuking because an apostasy is coming. Paul declares that he has fought the good fight and will receive his crown of righteousness. He asks Timothy to come to him and bring certain people who have remained loyal through his imprisonment. He prays that the Lord be with Timothy and ends the epistle.

- **Titus 1:**
  - **Before You Read:** Titus was a trusted companion of Paul's who had stood by his side through his imprisonment in Rome. This epistle was written as Titus remained in Crete, and contains some instructions for the church and personal messages for Titus. Look for JST in the footnotes.
  - **What You'll Read About:** Paul greets Titus and explains that he left Titus in Crete to ordain elders and organize the church there. He gives some qualifications for the elders and bishops Titus should call, including those who are blameless, temperate, and holding fast to faithful words. Paul describes some people who must be rebuked for deceiving and teaching for their own gain.

- **Titus 2:**
  - **Before You Read:** Paul has been writing to Titus with advice and instructions for the church in Crete.
  - **What You'll Read About:** Paul gives direction on what to teach different groups of people: old men and women, young men and women, and servants. He instructs Titus to show sincerity and good works so even his enemies will have reason to listen. Deny worldly lusts and live soberly and righteously. Paul testifies of Christ as the One who will redeem and purify us.

- **Titus 3:**
  - **Before You Read:** In the previous chapter, Paul wrote about certain things Titus should teach to the Cretians, including to live with soberness and temperance. This is the final chapter for Paul's epistle to Titus.
  - **What You'll Read About:** Paul directs Titus to teach the Cretians to be subject to the government and be meek in all things. Christ's mercy and grace will save us. Titus should do good works, but avoid foolish questions and arguments. He instructs Titus to meet him in Nicopolis and closes the epistle.

- **Philemon 1:**
  - **Before You Read:** Philemon was a Christian who lived in Colosse. Paul wrote this personal letter and sent it with Philemon's slave Onesimus who had robbed his master and ran away to Rome.
  - **What You'll Read About:** Paul greets Philemon and rejoices in his support and love. Paul explains that he met Onesimus in Rome, converted him, and is sending him back to Philemon. He asks Philemon to receive Onesimus again as a brother, and to fully forgive him. Paul writes that he will repay anything Philemon is owed, and closes his epistle.

SPIRITUAL GUIDING QUESTIONS

Question: How can you be a better example of the believers? (1 Timothy 4:12)

Question: How can you tell the difference between an anxious thought and a prompting from the Lord? (2 Timothy 1:7)

Question: What are some strategies you have developed for combating jealousy or pride in your financial situation? How can you feel more contentment? (1 Timothy 6:5-8)

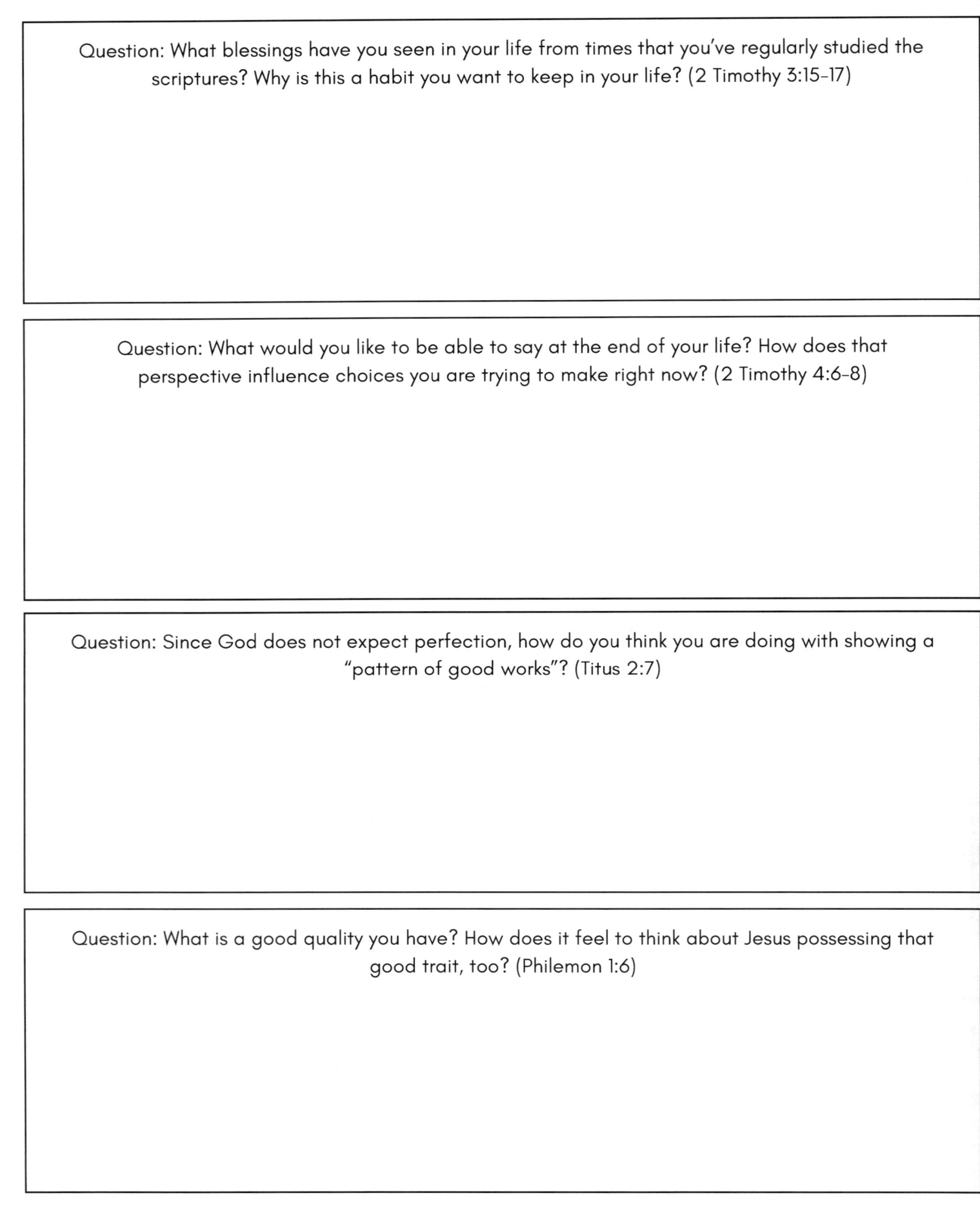

Question: What blessings have you seen in your life from times that you've regularly studied the scriptures? Why is this a habit you want to keep in your life? (2 Timothy 3:15-17)

Question: What would you like to be able to say at the end of your life? How does that perspective influence choices you are trying to make right now? (2 Timothy 4:6-8)

Question: Since God does not expect perfection, how do you think you are doing with showing a "pattern of good works"? (Titus 2:7)

Question: What is a good quality you have? How does it feel to think about Jesus possessing that good trait, too? (Philemon 1:6)

OCTOBER 30 - NOVEMBER 5

HEBREWS 1-6

"Jesus Christ 'the Author of Eternal Salvation'"

BIG PICTURE

How to feel confident fitting in this week's readings with the entire New Testament

General Context:

- **Are you ready for our study of the final Pauline epistle in the New Testament?** As we finish up the Pauline epistles (don't worry, we've still got a few more epistles from other people!), let's do a quick refresh of what Paul wrote. You may remember that Paul's epistles can be broken into 4 groupings:
  - **1 and 2 Thessalonians** were written in A.D. 50-51
  - **1 and 2 Corinthians, Galatians, and Romans** were written in A.D. 55-57
  - **Philippians, Colossians, Ephesians, Philemon, and Hebrews** were written in A.D. 60-62
  - **Titus, 1 and 2 Timothy** were written in A.D. 64-65
- **Remember, the epistles are arranged in order from longest to shortest within 3 categories:** Paul's epistles to churches, Paul's epistles to individuals, and epistles by other people. We've studied all of Paul's epistles to churches, and we just finished Paul's epistles to individuals so. . . Where did the book of Hebrews come from?! And why is it so long if we are going in length order?!
- **The short answer is that for a long time, people didn't know who wrote this epistle.** In fact, it is still widely debated whether or not Paul actually wrote Hebrews. Unlike his other epistles, he doesn't identify himself in the first few verses as being the author. That could be because this letter had a more specific purpose and was therefore more carefully planned out and written like a sermon. Some have speculated the author could actually be Luke, Silas, or Barnabas. But no matter who actually wrote this, the ideas are clearly in line with Paul's teachings. Because of the ambiguity of authorship, Hebrews, despite its length, is placed in between the Pauline epistles and the epistles written by other people. For ease, I will refer to Paul as the author of Hebrews in this study guide.

- **Well, whoever wrote it, why did the Hebrews get an epistle?** Hebrews, AKA Jews, were not limited to a single geographic location. So this epistle is unique because it is not written to a group of people in a specific area. Instead, it is written to all the Jews who were now in the Christian church. Remember the Jerusalem Council in A.D. 49? It was at this conference that church leaders determined new Gentile (non-Jew) converts did not need to follow the full Law of Moses. When Paul wrote this epistle to the Hebrews in A.D. 60, it had been about 10 years since this landmark decision that was only specifically about Gentiles. However, it had never officially been taught that Jews could stop their strict adherence to these laws! Many Jews still held on tight to their Law of Moses traditions.
- **What is in Hebrews?** In this carefully planned epistle, Paul explains to the Jews why they can let go of the Law of Moses and embrace Christ's gospel. You'll notice that Paul quotes extensively from Old Testament texts, which would make sense considering both Paul's past identity as a Pharisee, and his audience. The lessons and doctrines contained in Hebrews are considered among Paul's most significant. We will study Paul's powerful teachings to the Hebrews for the next two weeks!

Spiritual Themes:

Look for these themes as you read the chapters this week! Find examples in the scriptures, and ponder on what these themes can look like in your life.

- **Jesus Christ's Humanity and Divinity**

- **Diligence**

- **God's Rest**

People to Know:

- **Paul**
    - Paul (also known by his Hebrew name Saul) was a devout Jew and Pharisee. He was also a Roman citizen by birth. He persecuted the new Christian believers after Jesus' resurrection and ascension and was a strict believer in the Law of Moses. On his way to arrest more Christian believers, Paul was stopped on the road to Damascus and saw a vision of Jesus Christ. Paul was converted to Christianity and became a powerful missionary, spreading the gospel to many Gentiles. Paul served three big missionary trips that are recorded in the book of Acts (and possibly a fourth one later). He was ultimately martyred in Rome.

this week:
where are we?

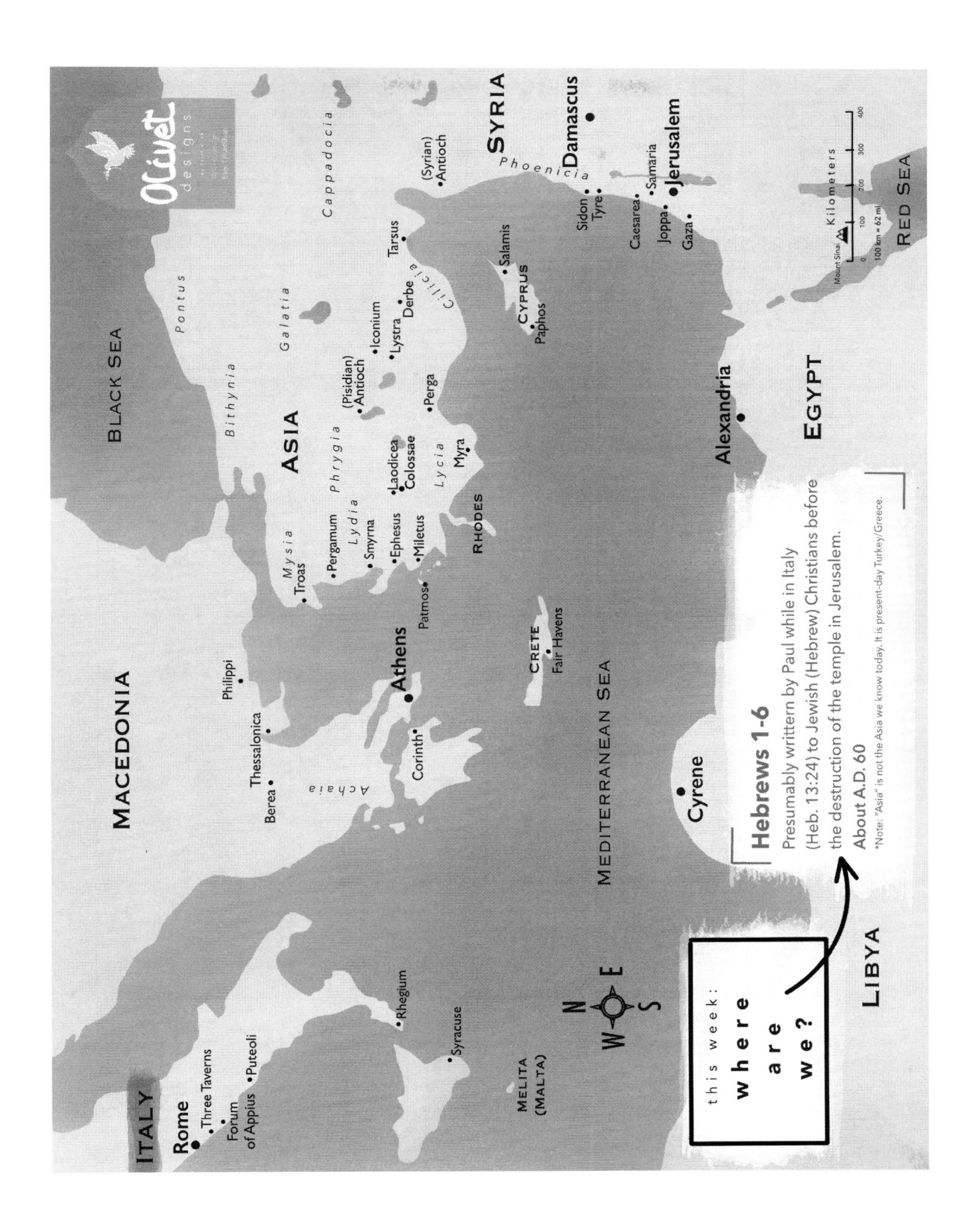

Hebrews 1-6

Presumably written by Paul while in Italy (Heb. 13:24) to Jewish (Hebrew) Christians before the destruction of the temple in Jerusalem.

About A.D. 60

*"Note: "Asia" is not the Asia we know today. It is present-day Turkey/Greece.

LITTLE PICTURE
How to understand each chapter and apply principles to my life

- **Hebrews 1:**
    - **Before You Read:** This epistle was written to Jews in the Christian church, and was meant to persuade them that they no longer needed to observe the Law of Moses. As this epistle begins, look for how Paul emphasizes Christ's glory and power. Look for JST in the footnotes.
    - **What You'll Read About:** Christ is the glorious creator who has purged our sins. Jesus is higher than the angels and has been anointed with the oil of gladness. Christ's power is eternal.

- **Hebrews 2:**
    - **Before You Read:** In the previous chapter, Paul emphasized Christ's great power and glory. When this chapter discusses bondage and the "word of angels", it's referencing the Law of Moses, which is lesser than Christ's law.
    - **What You'll Read About:** The Law of Moses (word of angels) worked well and had clear punishments, but our ultimate salvation is through Christ. Psalm 8 is quoted, and we learn that some have been valuing Christ's words and laws less than the Law of Moses. Through Christ's life and death we are sanctified and delivered from bondage. Christ became like man so he could understand our difficulties.

- **Hebrews 3:**
    - **Before You Read:** The previous chapter discussed the preeminence of Christ and His laws, and emphasized His role in our salvation. Remember this epistle is written to show Jews in the Christian church that they no longer need the strict Law of Moses.
    - **What You'll Read About:** Jesus Christ is our High Priest. As God's Son, He has even more glory than Moses, who is a servant. Do not harden our hearts, but exhort one another daily so you can be steadfast to the end. Paul warns against acting like the Hebrews who wandered 40 years in the wilderness because their hearts were hardened.

- **Hebrews 4:**
  - **Before You Read:** In the previous chapter, the Hebrews are warned against hardening their hearts.. Look for JST in both the footnotes and the Appendix.
  - **What You'll Read About:** If we receive the gospel without faith, we cannot enter into God's rest. God rested on the seventh day, and Jesus will give us rest if we believe and labor diligently. The word of God is quick, powerful, and sharp. Christ knows our temptations and infirmities, so come boldly to receive His grace.

- **Hebrews 5:**
  - **Before You Read:** The previous chapter testified of Christ's ability to give us rest if we have faith.
  - **What You'll Read About:** People who are ordained to the priesthood must be called of God, as was Aaron in Moses' day. Christ was called, and learned obedience through His suffering. Paul compares the readers to children in their understanding, counseling them to rely on milk instead of meat.

- **Hebrews 6:**
  - **Before You Read:** In the previous chapter, Paul taught about Christ's experience learning obedience and becoming the High Priest. Look for JST in the footnotes.
  - **What You'll Read About:** Let us go on to perfection with the principles of repentance, faith, baptism, laying on of hands, and the resurrection. Those who once were enlightened and then fall away crucify Christ anew. God sees our good works and ministering and will fulfill His promises to us. The hope we receive from God's promises can be an anchor for the soul.

SPIRITUAL GUIDING QUESTIONS

Question: When is a time that you had to completely trust the Lord? What did you learn from that experience? (Hebrews 2:13)

Question: Why is it important to know that Jesus understands temptation? What is a temptation you have overcome in your life? What is a temptation you still struggle with? (Hebrews 2:18)

Question: How have daily gospel habits benefitted your testimony? Why do you think daily rejuvenation is so essential? (Hebrews 3:13)

Question: What does it mean to you to "enter into" the Lord's rest? (Hebrews 4:3-5)

Question: How is the word of God "powerful" and "sharp"? When is a time you felt the piercing word of God enter your heart? (Hebrews 4:12)

Question: How could you approach God "boldly" but also humbly? When have you taken a bold question or request to the Lord? (Hebrews 4:16)

Question: How is the hope that God will keep His promises similar to an anchor for your soul? (Hebrews 6:19)

NOVEMBER 6 - NOVEMBER 12

HEBREWS 7-13

"An High Priest of Good Things to Come"

BIG PICTURE

How to feel confident fitting in this week's readings with the entire New Testament

General Context:

- **It's our second and final week in Paul's Epistle to the Hebrews.** This is the final Pauline epistle that we will study in the New Testament! Paul's authorship has been debated for centuries, but no matter who penned it, the ideas and convictions in Hebrews are absolutely Paul's. This epistle was likely written around A.D. 62, while Paul was imprisoned in Rome. You might remember that this was the same time period that Paul also wrote to the Ephesians, Philippians, Colossians, and Philemon.
- **Where were the Hebrews living?** That's the thing - "Hebrew" is just another name for "Jew". And the Jews were living everywhere! This makes Paul's epistle to the Hebrews unique, because Paul was writing to a large group of people who were not gathered in one geographical location.
- **Why did the Hebrews need an epistle?** It had been over 10 years since church leaders at the Jerusalem Council determined that Gentile (non-Jew) converts did NOT need to follow all of the Law of Moses. But this meant that within Christian congregations, there were groups of Jews, who strictly lived the Law of Moses, and Gentiles, who did not, trying to worship together. This inevitably led to the Jews believing that they were superior to the Gentile converts for still trying to follow this "higher" group of laws. Throughout Paul's epistle, he is clearly trying to make the point that the Law of Moses is actually the "lesser" law, and that Jesus Christ reigns supreme. You'll notice Paul's powerful teachings on Jesus that prove that following Christ, worshiping Him, having faith in Him, and staying diligent until the end is the highest and most holy way to live.

Spiritual Themes:

Look for these themes as you read the chapters this week! Find examples in the scriptures, and ponder on what these themes can look like in your life.

- **Faith in Jesus Christ**

- **The Higher Law**

- **Covenants**

People to Know:

- **Paul**
    - Paul (also known by his Hebrew name Saul) was a devout Jew and Pharisee. He was also a Roman citizen by birth. He persecuted the new Christian believers after Jesus' resurrection and ascension and was a strict believer in the Law of Moses. On his way to arrest more Christian believers, Paul was stopped on the road to Damascus and saw a vision of Jesus Christ. Paul was converted to Christianity and became a powerful missionary, spreading the gospel to many Gentiles. Paul served three big missionary trips that are recorded in the book of Acts (and possibly a fourth one later). He was ultimately martyred in Rome.

Hebrews 7-13

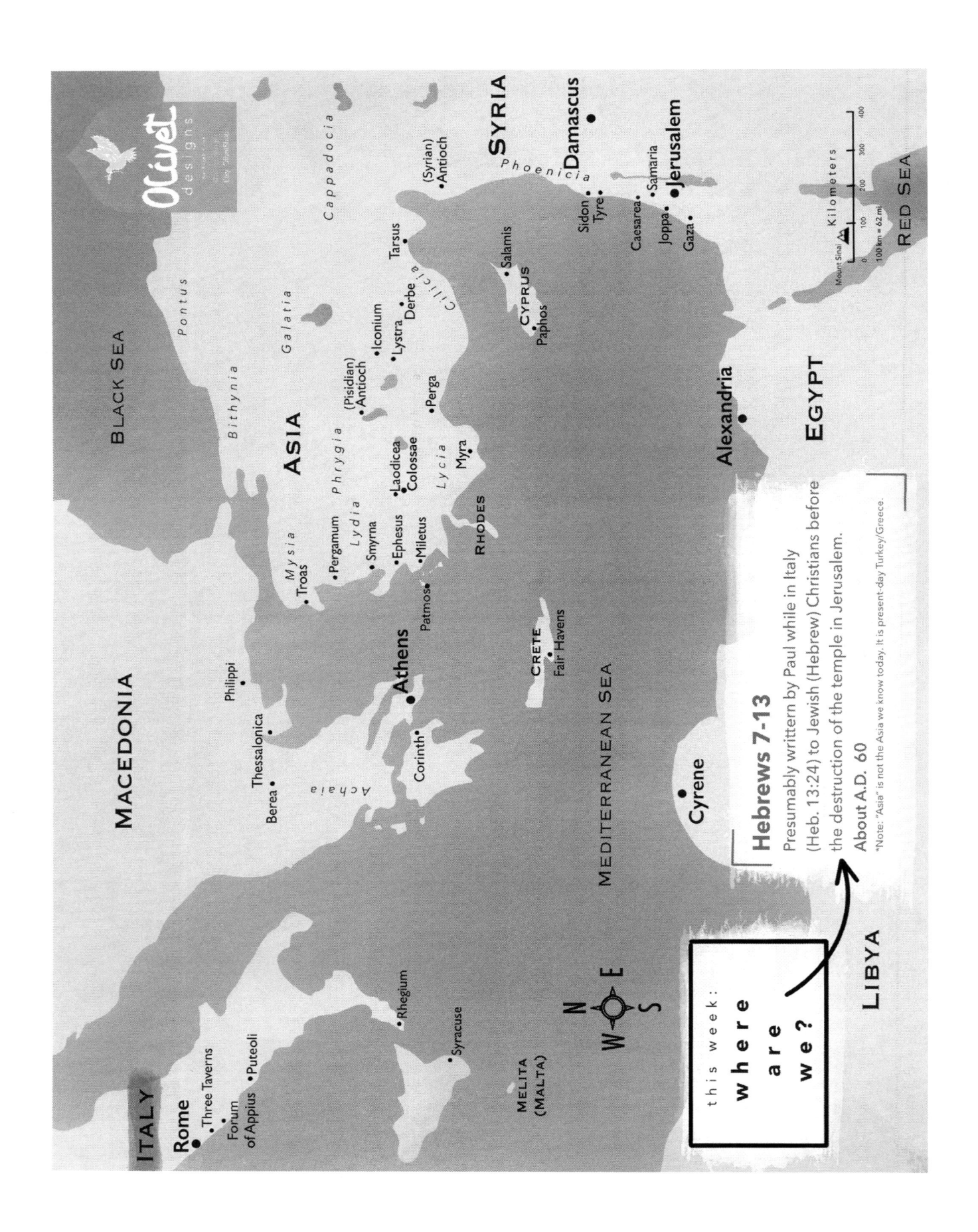

Presumably written by Paul while in Italy (Heb. 13:24) to Jewish (Hebrew) Christians before the destruction of the temple in Jerusalem.

About A.D. 60

*Note: "Asia" is not the Asia we know today. It is present-day Turkey/Greece.

this week: where are we?

LITTLE PICTURE
How to understand each chapter and apply principles to my life

- **Hebrews 7:**
  - **Before You Read:** In Hebrews 6, Paul taught that God keeps His promises, so we can rely on that hope when we are righteous. Remember that this epistle is written to the Jews in the Christian church, so it emphasizes Christ as the Savior, not the Law of Moses. Be sure to look at all three JST in the Appendix.
  - **What You'll Read About:** We learn about the life and greatness of the High Priest Melchizedek, who blessed Abraham and to whom Abraham paid tithes. Similarly, Levites receive tithes, though Levi himself would have given tithes to Abraham. Paul demonstrates that the priesthood of Melchizedek (in which Christ is the High Priest) is higher than the Levitical/Aaronic priesthood. Christ's eternal priesthood and hope can perfect us, while the law alone cannot. Christ is our perfect, holy High Priest who will not die, and has offered Himself as a sacrifice for our sins.

- **Hebrews 8:**
  - **Before You Read:** The previous chapter discussed the Melchizedek and Aaronic priesthoods. Look for JST in the footnotes.
  - **What You'll Read About:** Christ is our High Priest who has offered Himself as a sacrifice. Christ has created an even better covenant than the Law of Moses, which He will write in our hearts and minds. With this new covenant, the old can vanish away.

- **Hebrews 9:**
  - **Before You Read:** In the previous chapter, Paul showed that the Law of Moses is an old covenant that has been replaced by Christ's new laws. In this chapter, he will continue to show how the first covenant (Law of Moses) is swallowed up in Christ's law. Look for JST in the footnotes.
  - **What You'll Read About:** The tabernacle as used in the Law of Moses is described, with some of its symbols and ceremonies. Christ is the high priest of good things to come, and has built a more perfect (figurative) tabernacle where He has already obtained eternal salvation for us. Christ is the mediator of this new covenant, which He sealed with His blood.

- **Hebrews 10:**
  - **Before You Read:** The previous chapter taught us about the power of Christ shedding His own blood as a witness in His new testament and law. Look for JST in the footnotes.
  - **What You'll Read About:** The Law of Moses was a shadow of things to come, and the animal sacrifices do not take away sins. Christ came to offer His own body as a final sacrifice and establish a new law. If we have the law written in our hearts, we will receive a remission of our sins. We should hold fast to our faith, because we cannot be forgiven for willful sins. God will harshly judge those who do not honor Christ's sacrifice. Live with patience and faith and God will fulfill His promises.

- **Hebrews 11:**
  - **Before You Read:** The previous chapter showed the superiority of Christ's priesthood and gospel over the Law of Moses because of His eternal sacrifice. Look for JST in the footnotes.
  - **What You'll Read About:** Faith is the substance of things not seen. Paul gives examples of stories in the scriptures where people showed great faith, including Abraham, Sara, and Moses. People have always been able to make miracles happen through their faith in Jesus Christ and their promised blessings.

- **Hebrews 12:**
  - **Before You Read:** Hebrews 11 showed numerous examples of faith throughout the Old Testament, including Abraham, Sara, Isaac, Jacob, and Moses.
  - **What You'll Read About:** Having learned about all these witnesses, we must set aside sin and look to Jesus Christ for our salvation. God chastening us shows that He loves us and treats us as His children. Lift up hands that hang down and live with peace and holiness. Moses' experience getting the first law on Mount Sinai is compared to Christ being the mediator of the new law, which is for everybody.

- **Hebrews 13:**
  - **Before You Read:** The previous chapter taught about Christ as the mediator of the new law and explained that God chastens us because He loves us. This is the final chapter in the epistle.
  - **What You'll Read About:** Be loving to all, including strangers and those in bondage. Marriage is honorable and Christ is the same forever. Christ suffered and sacrificed Himself for us. We should praise God and do good continually. Obey and pray for your honest leaders.

SPIRITUAL GUIDING QUESTIONS

Question: What does the Lord do when we repent? How has repentance been a meaningful gift in your life? (Hebrews 8:12)

Question: What does it mean to you that Christ is the "high priest of good things to come"? (Hebrews 9:11)

Question: What do you think the difference is between "blind faith" and "full assurance of faith"? (Hebrews 10:22)

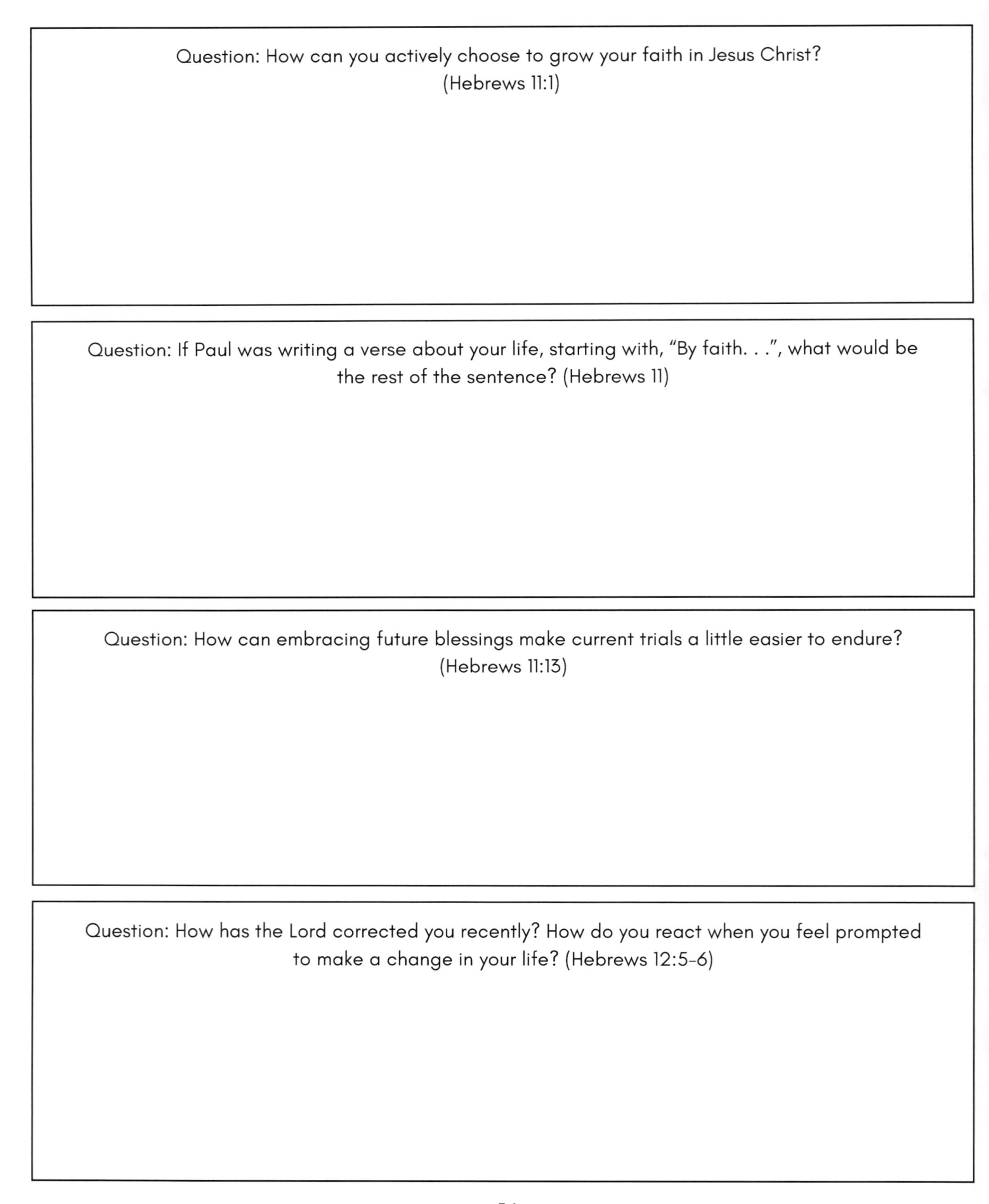

Question: How can you actively choose to grow your faith in Jesus Christ?
(Hebrews 11:1)

Question: If Paul was writing a verse about your life, starting with, "By faith. . .", what would be the rest of the sentence? (Hebrews 11)

Question: How can embracing future blessings make current trials a little easier to endure?
(Hebrews 11:13)

Question: How has the Lord corrected you recently? How do you react when you feel prompted to make a change in your life? (Hebrews 12:5-6)

NOVEMBER 13 - NOVEMBER 19

JAMES 1-5

"Be Ye Doers of the Word, and Not Hearers Only"

BIG PICTURE

How to feel confident fitting in this week's readings with the entire New Testament

General Context:

- **We are leaving the Pauline epistles behind and jumping into the "general epistles".** The general epistles are letters that were written by various church leaders to the entire church body in general – not a specific location like many of Paul's letters.
    - **The general epistles are: James, 1 Peter, 2 Peter, 1 John, 2 John, 3 John, and Jude.**
    - **They are arranged by length** from longest to shortest, NOT chronologically.
- **Who is James?** This week, we are studying the General Epistle of James. James is the half-brother of Jesus Christ and the son of Mary and Joseph. He was not converted to the gospel until after Jesus' resurrection. However, he soon became a powerful and active leader in the church! As a church leader, James very likely wrote this epistle from Jerusalem to the general church. It is difficult to determine when James wrote this, but it is possible that it is the earliest out of all the New Testament books, likely between A.D. 45-50. To keep things in perspective, Paul's earliest epistle to the Thessalonians was written in A.D. 50.
- **Why did James write this?** Since this is a general epistle, James is addressing the church membership at large. He includes doctrinal truths and administrative advice that he wanted to share. Look for references to Jesus' Sermon on the Mount, as many scholars have noted this epistle may have been James' response to and elaboration on Jesus' famous teachings.
- **And we have to mention Joseph Smith!** The verses that set the Restoration of the Gospel of Jesus Christ into motion were found by young Joseph Smith in James 1:5-6. In fact, some have called these verses the most important verses in the entire Bible because they inspired young Joseph to ask a question that led to the Restoration of the fullness of the Gospel of Jesus Christ.

Spiritual Themes:

Look for these themes as you read the chapters this week! Find examples in the scriptures, and ponder on what these themes can look like in your life.

- **Good Works**

- **Asking God**

- **God's Wisdom**

People to Know:

- **James**
    - Also known as "James the Just", James was the half-brother of Jesus Christ, the son of Mary and Joseph. As Jesus Himself referred to many times during His mortal ministry, it seemed as though His own family did not believe in His divinity and mission, and James was no exception. However, after Jesus' resurrection, James became fully converted to the gospel and to Christianity. James became a faithful and powerful church leader in Jerusalem. He wrote an epistle to the church membership in general expounding on the Savior's teachings. He was likely martyred around A.D. 62.

James

An epistle to the 12 tribes of Israel, written by James, the half brother of Christ, and first Bishop of the Church in Jerusalem. About A.D. 45-60, before James was stoned to death in A.D. 62.

*Note: "Asia" is not the Asia we know today. It is present-day Turkey/Greece.

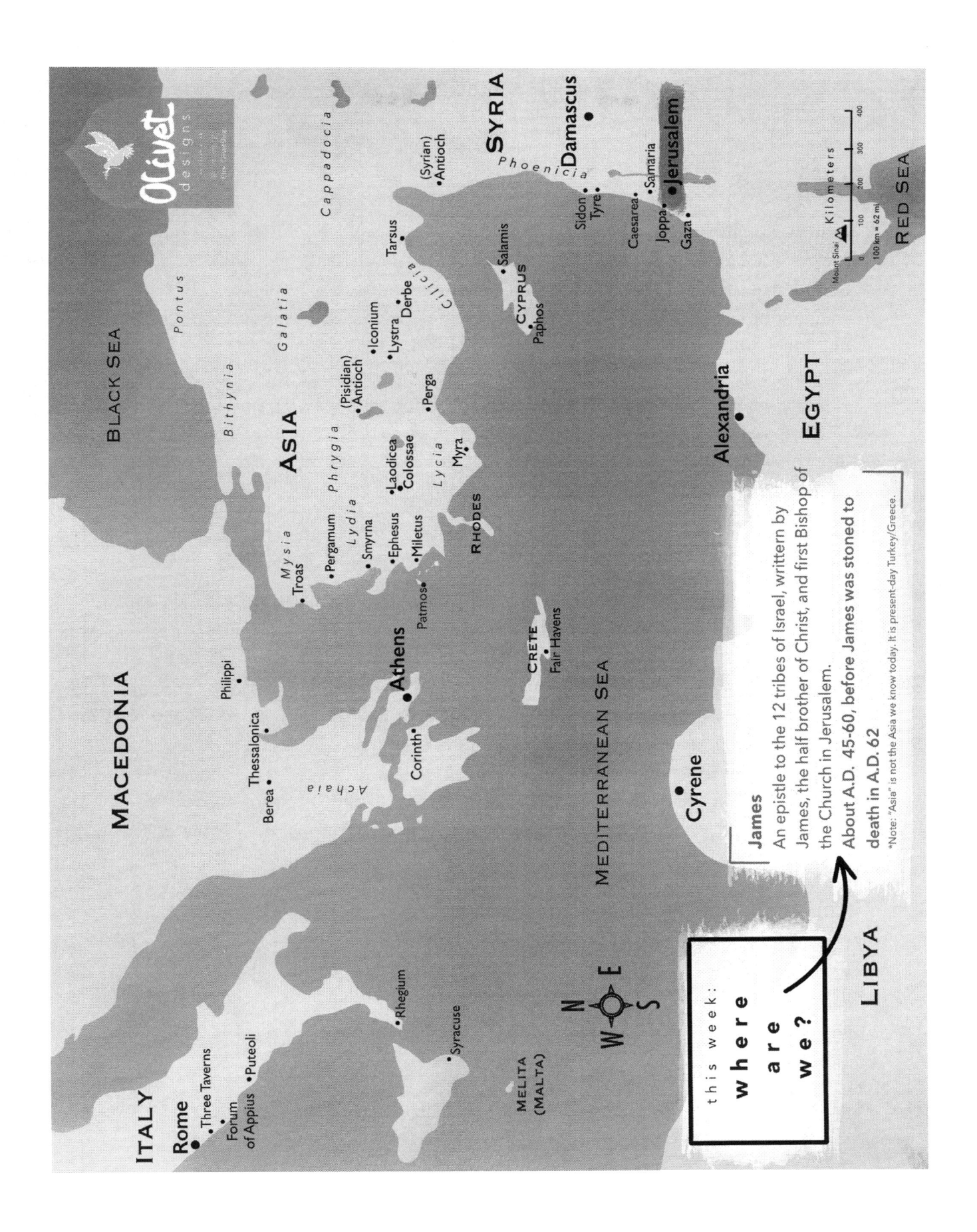

this week: **where are we?**

LITTLE PICTURE
How to understand each chapter and apply principles to my life

- **James 1:**
  - **Before You Read:** This epistle was written by James, church leader and half-brother to Jesus. It's a general epistle, so instead of Paul's epistles which always had specific audiences, this one was written to the church membership in general. Look for the verses that inspired Joseph Smith to ask God his own questions at the beginning of the Restoration. Look for JST in the footnotes.
  - **What You'll Read About:** If you lack wisdom, ask God with faith and He will answer you. Riches will fade, but blessed is he that endures temptation and lust. Every good gift comes from God. Avoid wrath and filthiness, and receive God's word with meekness. Don't just hear God's word, but do it too. Pure religion is visiting the fatherless and widows.

- **James 2:**
  - **Before You Read:** In the previous chapter, James gave many bits of doctrine and advice, and taught that true religion is serving and visiting the fatherless and widows. Look for JST in the footnotes and the Appendix.
  - **What You'll Read About:** Do not judge people based on their wealth, because God has chosen the poor to be rich in faith. In order to be fully blameless, we cannot obey most of the law and break just one commandment. We can't have faith without works, but our faith should show through our good works.

- **James 3:**
  - **Before You Read:** In the previous chapter, James taught that faith without works is dead, and showed that we can show faith through our works. Be sure to check out the JST in the first verse of this chapter.
  - **What You'll Read About:** We must learn to bridle our tongues so that we do not offend others. Our tongues are powerful, able to both bless and curse. Worldly wisdom leads to confusion and evil, but wisdom from above is pure and leads to mercy and peace.

- **James 4:**
  - **Before You Read:** James has been writing about the importance of controlling our speech and pursuing godly wisdom.
  - **What You'll Read About:** Lusting and covetousness lead to wars and adultery. A friend of the world is an enemy to God, but God gives grace to the humble. If we draw near to God and He will draw near to us. Our afflictions and mourning humble us and bring us closer to God. Do not judge one another. Life is fleeting, so if we know to do good, do good.

- **James 5:**
  - **Before You Read:** James has been writing in this epistle his teachings on how to be a faithful follower of Christ. He wrote in the previous chapter about the importance of humbling yourself so that God can lift you up. This is the final chapter in the epistle.
  - **What You'll Read About:** James writes about the misery that awaits the unrighteous rich, because their riches will fade, but their unjust actions will not. Be patient, and remember that those who suffer (like Job) will be blessed for their endurance. If you are sick, call the elders for a blessing. A fervent prayer brings blessings. Converting a sinner saves a soul from death.

SPIRITUAL GUIDING QUESTIONS

Question: What is a question on your heart right now? What could you learn from Joseph Smith's example of how he asked his question? (James 1:5)

Question: When is a time that you listened to a talk, lesson, or scripture and then actively chose to make a change as a result of what you learned? (James 1:22)

Question: Why is charity such an integral part of Christ's gospel? Who has shown you charity recently? (James 1:27)

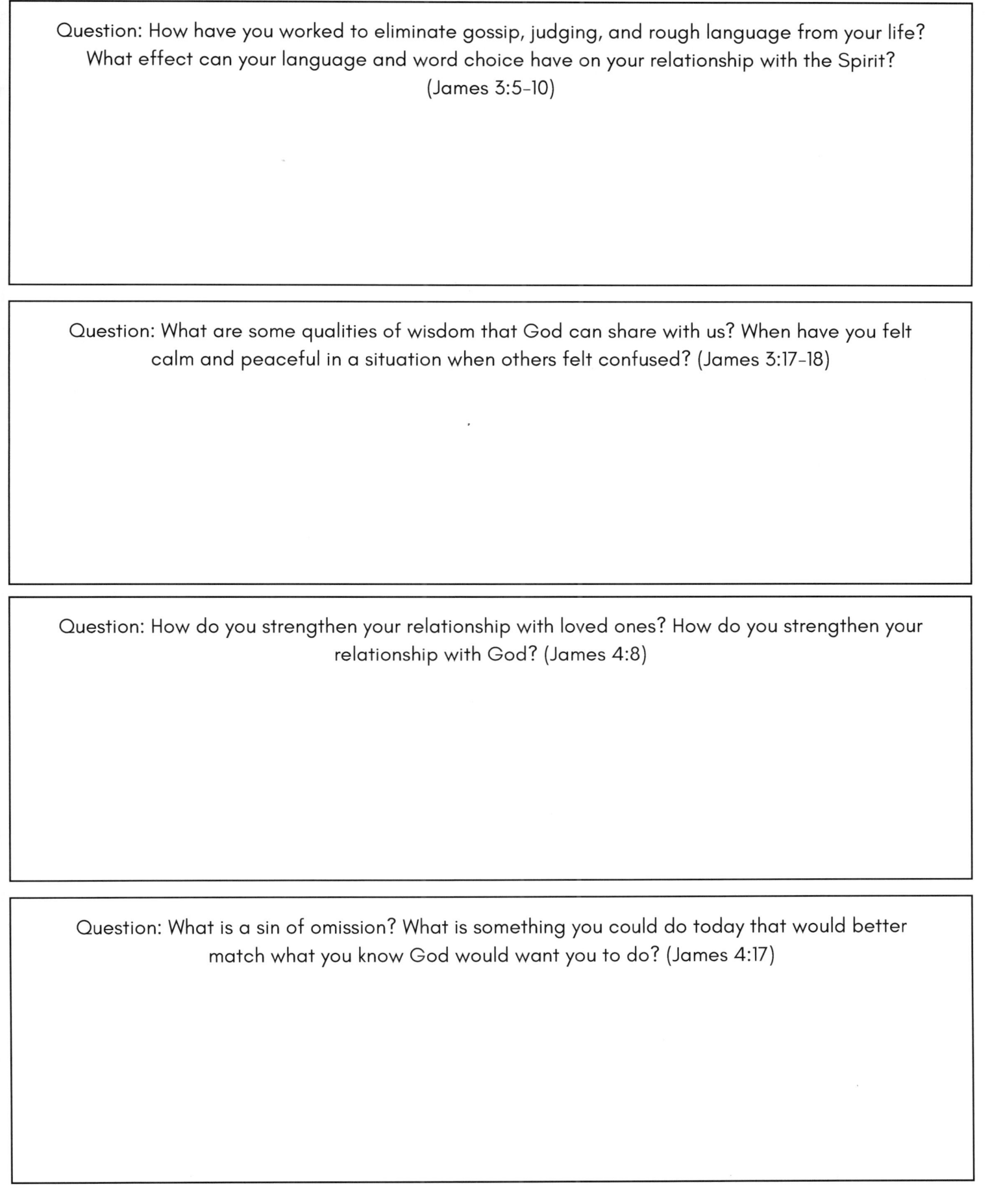

Question: How have you worked to eliminate gossip, judging, and rough language from your life? What effect can your language and word choice have on your relationship with the Spirit?
(James 3:5-10)

Question: What are some qualities of wisdom that God can share with us? When have you felt calm and peaceful in a situation when others felt confused? (James 3:17-18)

Question: How do you strengthen your relationship with loved ones? How do you strengthen your relationship with God? (James 4:8)

Question: What is a sin of omission? What is something you could do today that would better match what you know God would want you to do? (James 4:17)

NOVEMBER 20 - NOVEMBER 26

1 AND 2 PETER

"Rejoice with Joy Unspeakable and Full of Glory"

BIG PICTURE

How to feel confident fitting in this week's readings with the entire New Testament

General Context:

- **It's been a while since we talked about Peter!** This week, we will study the 2 epistles that Peter wrote. We are continuing on with the general epistles, which are the epistles written by various leaders to the church membership at large.

- **Peter has been involved since the very beginning of the New Testament.** You'll remember that Peter was called by Jesus to be a disciple. Peter had some rough times (like denying Jesus) and some amazing times (like witnessing the Mount of Transfiguration). By the time of Jesus' crucifixion and resurrection, Peter became the Chief Apostle and the one who held all of the priesthood keys. He traveled around to various cities, and also presided over official church business in Jerusalem. We have 2 epistles that Peter wrote, and both are at the very end of Peter's life. It is widely accepted that Peter was martyred in Rome around A.D. 66.

- **The first epistle of Peter was written while Peter was with Silas and John Mark.** They were in Rome at the time, likely A.D. 64, although Peter calls Rome the shaded code name "Babylon". Nero had just become the Roman Emperor and he was persecuting all the Christians. While many of the Jewish Christians were used to persecution, the newly converted Gentile Christians were struggling with this new weight of deciding whether or not to deny their beliefs for their ease of life. As you read 1 Peter, look for how Peter tries to support the Gentile Christians by encouraging them to be strong in the faith, even when faced with opposition.
  - **As a fun connection:** You'll remember that when we studied the four Gospels, we learned that John Mark was the author of the book of Mark. But Mark never even saw Jesus! How did Mark know anything about the details of Jesus Christ's mortal ministry?! The most believable answer comes from this time that John Mark and Peter spent together in Rome! It is widely accepted that Mark wrote his gospel account at the request of Peter, using Peter's intimate knowledge of the Lord's ministry. Since Mark's account seems to be the "source material" for Matthew and Luke, they likely read Mark's account of Peter's words, and then added details they felt their audiences would want to know (Matthew to the Jews and Luke to the educated Gentiles). John's Gospel account is almost completely unique, so he likely wrote it independently of Peter/Mark's account.

- **Peter's second epistle was written shortly before Peter's martyrdom, likely around A.D. 66.** This epistle was written to the same group of Gentile Christian churches as his first epistle. It was at this time that Peter started speaking more openly of the apostasy that was about to come. In his second epistle, you'll see Peter's clear and forward messaging about what the saints need to do in order to be saved.
    - **Did Jude plagiarize Peter?!** We won't study Jude's epistle until next week, but you may notice that Chapter 2 in Peter's second epistle is pretty similar to the entirety of Jude's epistle. Most scholars actually believe that Jude's epistle was written first. It seems plausible that Peter saw Jude's epistle and loved the message so much that he wanted to share it with more people. He likely wrote his own words for an introduction (Chapter 1), reworded Jude's message (Chapter 2), and then concluded with his own words (Chapter 3).

Spiritual Themes:

Look for these themes as you read the chapters this week! Find examples in the scriptures, and ponder on what these themes can look like in your life.

- **Righteous Suffering**

- **Good Works**

- **Humility**

People to Know:

- **Peter/Simon Peter**
    - Simon Peter, also known as just Peter, was one of the first disciples of Jesus. He was introduced to Jesus through his brother Andrew. Jesus gave Simon the new name of "Cephas" meaning "rock", which is the Aramaic version of the Greek name "Peter". Peter was a fisherman by trade. Peter became one of the three apostles closest to the Savior, including being a witness on the Mount of Transfiguration and in the Garden of Gethsemane. Peter seemed to have a bit of a rash and energetic side to him, being the apostle who wanted to walk on water, tried to rebuke Jesus, and cut off the ear of a soldier. After Jesus' resurrection, Peter became instrumental in taking the gospel to many different people. He became the Chief Apostle and held all of the priesthood keys. He was ultimately martyred upside down on a cross in Rome around A.D. 66.

- **Silas/Silvanus**
    - Silas was one of the church leaders in Jerusalem who was sent to Antioch with Judas, Paul, and Barnabas with the official word that new Gentile converts did not need to fully follow the Law of Moses. Silas then became Paul's new missionary companion, and they departed on Paul's second mission together. Silas served with both Paul and Peter, accompanying Peter in Rome when he wrote his first epistle.
- **John Mark/Marcus**
    - John Mark's mother Mary shared her home as a place for the Christians to gather and pray for Peter's release from prison. John Mark was Barnabas' cousin and accompanied Barnabas and Paul for a short duration of their first mission trip. However, John Mark left for unknown reasons in the middle of the mission, prompting contention between himself and Paul. Later, Barnabas requested John Mark come on the second mission trip with Paul, but Paul refused, causing Barnabas and John Mark to be companions on their own separate journey. John Mark would later reconcile with Paul and become a dear friend and strong member. He also accompanied Peter on some of his travels, eventually spending a lot of time with Peter in Rome. John Mark would write the Gospel of Mark, presumably at the request of and including the details from Peter.

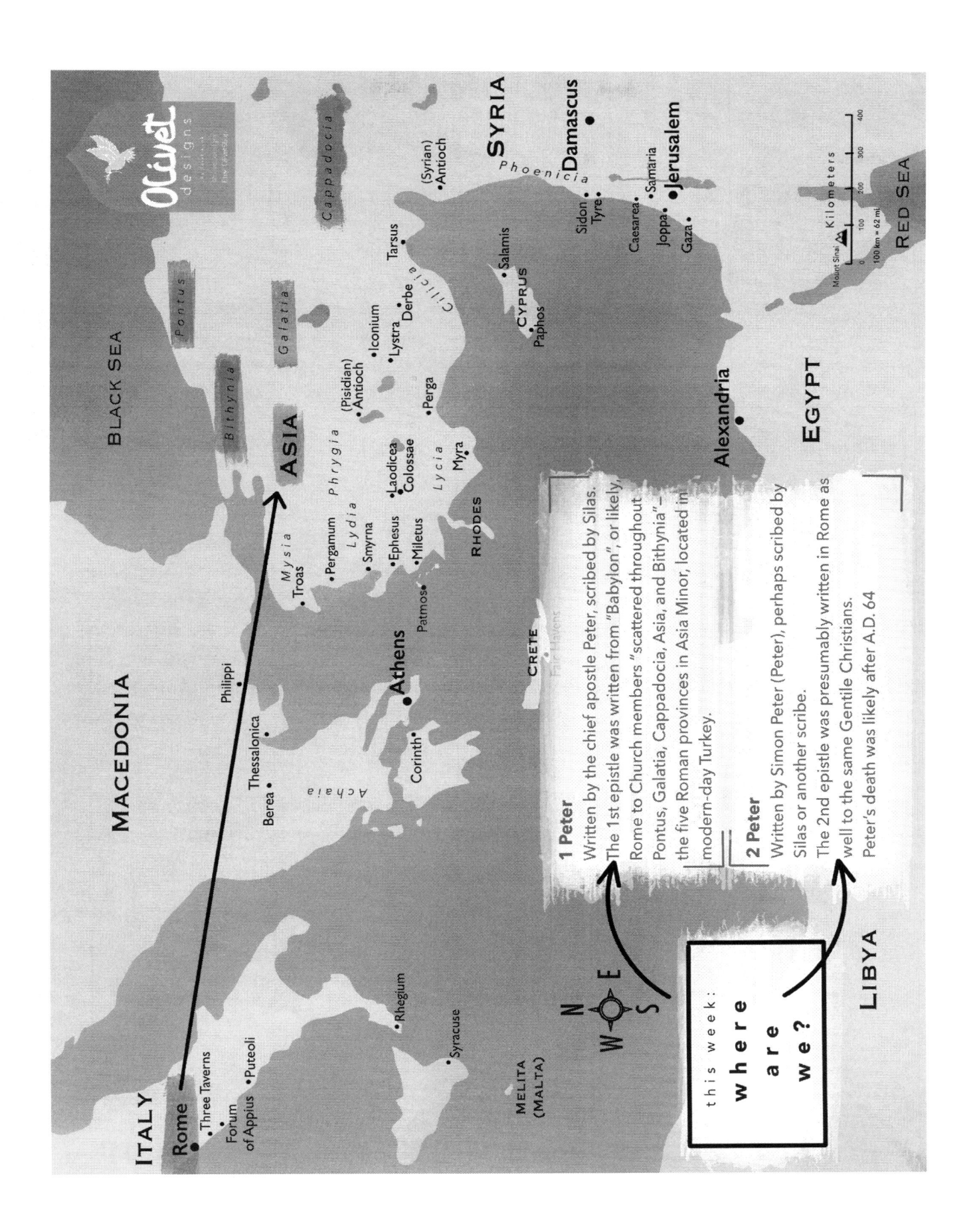

1 Peter
Written by the chief apostle Peter, scribed by Silas. The 1st epistle was written from "Babylon", or likely, Rome to Church members "scattered throughout Pontus, Galatia, Cappadocia, Asia, and Bithynia" – the five Roman provinces in Asia Minor, located in modern-day Turkey.

2 Peter
Written by Simon Peter (Peter), perhaps scribed by Silas or another scribe. The 2nd epistle was presumably written in Rome as well to the same Gentile Christians. Peter's death was likely after A.D. 64

this week: **where are we?**

LITTLE PICTURE
How to understand each chapter and apply principles to my life

- **1 Peter 1:**
  - **Before You Read:** This epistle written by Peter was addressed to Christians who were facing persecution under the reign of Nero. It was meant to both instruct them and encourage them to be strong in their faith. Look for JST in the footnotes.
  - **What You'll Read About:** Peter greets the saints in Asia Minor and praises the goodness and mercy of Jesus Christ. Their faith is being tried, but this trial will lead to glory at Christ's second coming. Be obedient and holy, for God judges us according to our works. We are redeemed through Christ's blood. Our lives pass away, but God's word endures forever.

- **1 Peter 2:**
  - **Before You Read:** In the previous chapter, Peter emphasized the eternal glory that following Christ brings. Remember that this epistle was written to saints who were being persecuted and even killed for their beliefs.
  - **What You'll Read About:** Peter compares becoming a new man in Christ to being born and desiring milk. Christ can be our chief cornerstone, but also a stumbling block to those who do not believe. Peter writes that they are a chosen generation, and teaches to avoid lust. Be subject to the government, and live in a way that others can see your faith. We receive glory when we patiently endure wrongful suffering, for Christ is our ultimate example in that.

- **1 Peter 3:**
  - **Before You Read:** Peter has been writing about the glory we can receive by suffering for our faith, which many of the saints he was writing to were experiencing. Look for JST in the footnotes.
  - **What You'll Read About:** Wives and husbands should honor one another. We all must be unified in one mind with compassion and peace, not speaking evil. If we suffer for the sake of righteousness, we are happy and do not need to fear. Christ suffered for our sins, then preached to the spirits in spirit prison following His death.

- **1 Peter 4:**
  - **Before You Read:** In the previous chapter, Peter taught about the joy that can come from being like Christ while suffering for righteousness. Look for JST in the footnotes.
  - **What You'll Read About:** Peter teaches that if we suffer, we should remain faithful and refrain from sin. He explains that the gospel is preached to the dead so that they can be fairly judged. He teaches to have charity, hospitality, and to speak with the spirit. We should rejoice in our righteous sufferings because it brings us closer to Christ.

- **1 Peter 5:**
  - **Before You Read:** In the previous chapter, Peter wrote about the joy and glory that can come from righteous suffering. Remember this epistle was written to people who were suffering and being persecuted for their faith. This is the final chapter of this epistle.
  - **What You'll Read About:** Peter gives direction to the elders of the church to feed their flocks and be examples to them. Be humble, sober, vigilant, and steadfast in the faith. Peter gives glory to God and closes his epistle.
- **2 Peter 1:**
  - **Before You Read:** This second epistle was addressed to the same group of churches in Asia Minor as the first, and its purpose is to try to clearly teach what the Christians needed to be doing in their lives to obtain salvation. Look for JST in the footnotes.
  - **What You'll Read About:** Christ has given us precious promises to escape the corruption and lust of the world. Peter lists qualities we should abound in to become fruitful in our faith. Work to ensure our own calling and election. Peter prophesies his own death, and writes about being on the Mount of Transfiguration with Christ. He teaches that prophecy comes from the power of the Holy Ghost.
- **2 Peter 2:**
  - **Before You Read:** Peter has been writing about how saints can abound in knowledge of the Savior, and that prophecy comes from the Holy Ghost. Note that the words in this chapter are almost entirely the same as the Epistle of Jude. It is probable that Jude wrote his epistle, and Peter wanted to share that same message with a broader audience.
  - **What You'll Read About:** There will be false teachers who try to deceive, but they will be destroyed. Peter gives examples of Old Testament people, including Noah and Lot, who were spared from destruction for their righteousness, and teaches that God will deliver us out of temptations. People who give in to the natural man will receive their judgment. It is worse to turn away from the truth after we know it than to have been ignorant all along.
- **2 Peter 3:**
  - **Before You Read:** Peter has been writing to members in various cities to inspire them to stay true to their faith, even in trials and persecutions. This is the final chapter in Peter's second epistle, and the final words that we have recorded from Peter. Look for JST in this chapter.
  - **What You'll Read About:** Peter writes that in the last days, people will doubt Christ's Second Coming and walk after their own lusts. Time is different to us than to God. We must be holy and godly because God will keep His promises, and Christ will come again like a thief in the night. Be steadfast and grow in grace and the knowledge of the Lord.

SPIRITUAL GUIDING QUESTIONS

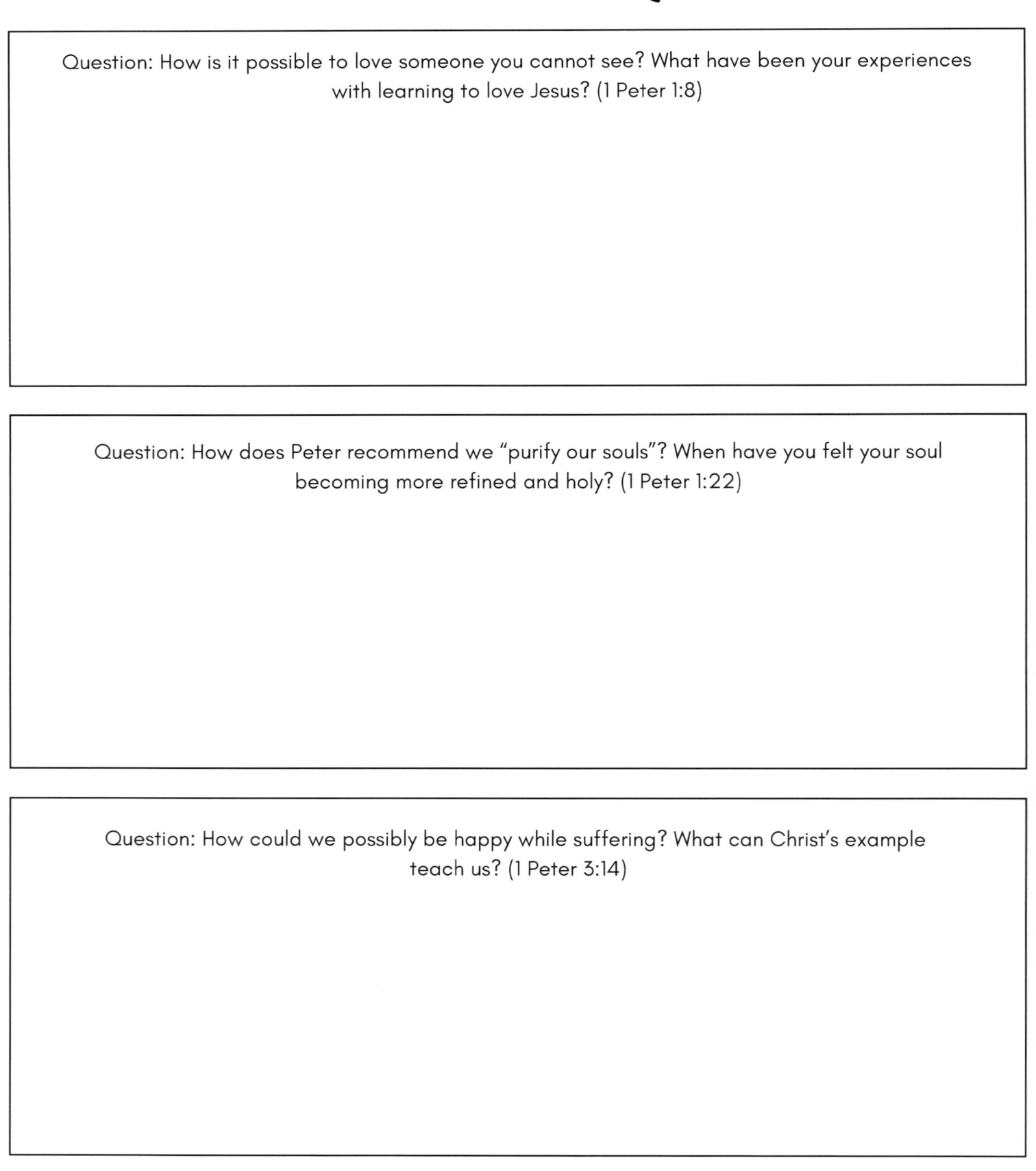

Question: How is it possible to love someone you cannot see? What have been your experiences with learning to love Jesus? (1 Peter 1:8)

Question: How does Peter recommend we "purify our souls"? When have you felt your soul becoming more refined and holy? (1 Peter 1:22)

Question: How could we possibly be happy while suffering? What can Christ's example teach us? (1 Peter 3:14)

Question: Why is it important to know that nothing has "gone wrong" when we experience trials? (1 Peter 4:12-13)

Question: Who do you have stewardship over, whether in your family or in a church calling? How can you be a better example to them? (1 Peter 5:2-3)

Question: Peter lists qualities that can help us be fruitful in our knowledge of Christ. How would your life be different if each of the qualities Peter lists truly abounded in you? (2 Peter 1:5-8)

Question: What are some ways you have grown spiritually in the last year? What ways do you look forward to growing in the future? (2 Peter 3:18)

NOVEMBER 27 - DECEMBER 3

1 - 3 JOHN; JUDE

"God Is Love"

BIG PICTURE

How to feel confident fitting in this week's readings with the entire New Testament

General Context:

- **Here we are, studying the final epistles in the New Testament!** The four epistles we will study this week, three from John and one from Jude, are still considered "general epistles". Even though some of them mention specific recipients, the doctrine and warnings found in each epistle are given to everyone.
- **Let's start with the three epistles that John wrote.** First of all, the author of these three epistles never specifically identifies himself, but it is widely accepted that John was the author. The writing style totally fits with the Gospel of John. Remember that this is the same John who wrote the Gospel of John, was a chief apostle to Jesus Christ, and the author of the Book of Revelation (which we will get to next week).
- **We know remarkably little about what John was doing after Jesus' resurrection,** other than a few references by Paul that he had spoken with John in Jerusalem. It seems like John made Ephesus his home base at some point, preaching and becoming familiar with the saints there. While the location of the recipients of John's epistles is never named, it is likely that they were intended for the Ephesians and addressed issues they were experiencing. We also don't have a great timeline for when these epistles were written.
    - **John's first epistle is a general epistle,** addressed to Christians in general. His longest epistle, John warns the Christians about some schisms that were occurring among their own congregations about whether or not Christ had an actual body of flesh. Some, influenced by popular philosophy at the time, reasoned that if Jesus were divine, He could not have had a body of flesh and blood, and they were preaching this with certainty. John corrects and rebukes these false preachers, and gives Christians guidelines for finding true doctrine.
    - **John's second epistle is addressed to an "elect lady".** We don't know who this elect lady is, so while there is technically a specific audience for this letter, it is still considered a "general epistle". In this epistle, John refers to himself as "the elder". John continues to address this schism around whether or not Jesus had a body of flesh and blood, and John says he hopes to visit the saints soon.

- ○ **The third epistle of John is addressed to Gaius**. Unfortunately, we don't know who Gaius was, as well as a few other names mentioned in this epistle. However, we can infer that Gaius and Demetrius were faithful saints who taught correct doctrine, and Diotrephes held a position of power in the church but denied that Jesus had a body of flesh and blood. John shows a genuine concern for the people, and fears they will fall into apostasy.
- **And what about Jude's epistle? Who was he?** In this epistle, Jude says he is a brother of James, whose epistle we studied last week, and who we know is half-brother to Jesus Christ (a child of Mary and Joseph). When Jesus' siblings are listed in the Gospels, there is also someone named "Juda" or "Judas" listed. We can safely assume then that Jude is also a brother of Jesus! We know nothing about what Jude had been doing since Christ's resurrection, but tradition has most of Jesus' family remaining in Galilee and becoming church leaders there. We also don't have any dates for when Jude may have written his epistle, although you may remember that Jude's epistle and part of Peter's 2nd epistle are very similar. This makes it likely that Jude wrote his epistle before Peter's 2nd epistle, assuming that Peter read Jude's epistle and wanted to share that same message with his audience.
- **What is Jude's epistle about?** This epistle is a general epistle, but was mainly addressed to Christians who were in danger of following other believers who had returned to Pagan worship. This epistle has many concepts and references to doctrines clarified in the Latter-Days, such as the war in heaven, the archangel Michael, and prophecies of Enoch.

Spiritual Themes:

Look for these themes as you read the chapters this week! Find examples in the scriptures, and ponder on what these themes can look like in your life.

- **Love One Another**

- **Jesus is Mortal and Divine**

- **Walk in the Light**

People to Know:

- **John**
  - John was one of Jesus Christ's original apostles. John was among the few who knew Jesus the best, along with Peter and John's brother James. They were the only 3 who saw Jesus raise Jairus' daughter from the dead and the only ones who were on the Mount of Transfiguration with Jesus. John had been a fisherman by trade and the Savior referred to John and his brother James as the "sons of thunder". After Christ's death, John ministered with Peter and spent a lot of time in Ephesus. He was eventually exiled to the island Patmos, which is where he received the vision contained in Revelation. Many other Christians believe that John is likely the only of the original apostles who died of old age (as opposed to martyrdom). However, revelation in both the Book of Mormon and the Doctrine and Covenants clarify that John has been allowed to remain on the earth as a ministering servant. (Check out 3 Nephi 28:6 and D&C 7 for more info on that!)
- **Jude**
  - Jude was the half-brother of Jesus Christ. He was also the brother of James, who wrote the epistle of James. Jude/Juda/Judas is listed as one of Jesus' siblings in Mark 6:3 and Matthew 13:55. While not much is known about Jude's life, it can be inferred that he was not a believer during Jesus' mortal ministry, but became converted after Christ's resurrection. He likely stayed in Galilee with other family members and became a church leader.

this week: where are we?

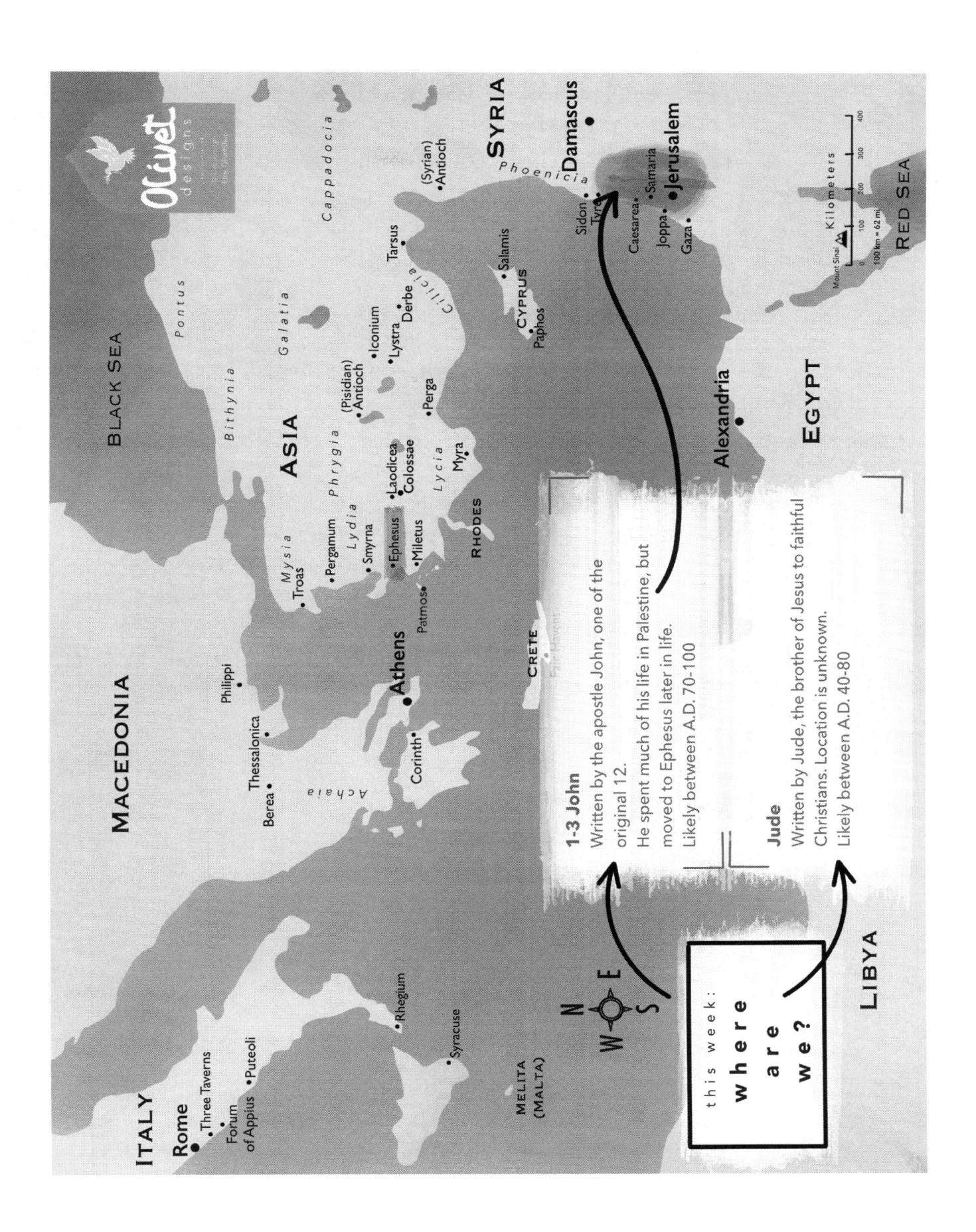

1-3 John
Written by the apostle John, one of the original 12.
He spent much of his life in Palestine, but moved to Ephesus later in life.
Likely between A.D. 70-100

Jude
Written by Jude, the brother of Jesus to faithful Christians. Location is unknown.
Likely between A.D. 40-80

LITTLE PICTURE
How to understand each chapter and apply principles to my life

- **1 John 1:**
  - **Before You Read:** This epistle was written by John who was an apostle to Jesus Christ. He wrote it to the church in general. It is meant to bolster faith in Christ's physical resurrection and generally assumes the reader has the knowledge of Jesus' mortal ministry. Look for JST in the footnotes.
  - **What You'll Read About:** John opens by testifying of Jesus Christ, and says that he writes this epistle to bring joy. If we walk in the light, Christ's blood will cleanse us. We must confess our sins to receive forgiveness.

- **1 John 2:**
  - **Before You Read:** In the previous chapter, John taught that we can receive forgiveness through Christ's blood. Look for JST in the footnotes.
  - **What You'll Read About:** Christ is our advocate if we sin. We can only truly know Christ by keeping His commandments. If we love one another, we walk in the light. Do not love the lusts of the world, for the world will pass away. Antichrists have come, but we should keep the same knowledge of Jesus Christ that we've always had. Abide in Christ and be born of Him in righteousness, so that we will be ready for His coming.

- **1 John 3:**
  - **Before You Read:** John has been writing about antichrists coming and that we should walk in the light of truth. Look for JST in the footnotes.
  - **What You'll Read About:** We are the children of God, so we can become like Him. We can abide in Christ through righteousness, but sin separates us from Him. We must also love one another, for God already showed us ultimate love by dying for us. If we keep God's commandments, love one another, and believe in Christ, He will abide in us.

- **1 John 4:**
  - **Before You Read:** The previous chapter focused on what we need to do to have Christ abide in us, including loving others and keeping the commandments. Look for JST in the footnotes.
  - **What You'll Read About:** People with good spirits will testify of Jesus Christ as the Son of God. We are born of God when we become His and love one another. God is love, and He sent His Son to die for our sins. Perfect love casteth out fear. Love God and love our brother.

- **1 John 5:**
  - **Before You Read:** The previous chapter was all about love - God loved us so He sent His son, and we are commanded to love God and others. This is the final chapter of John's First Epistle.
  - **What You'll Read About:** We know that we are born of God when we love God and keep His commandments. John writes about witnesses in heaven and on earth, and that the people who believe receive their own witness. God will give us the righteous things we ask for. When we are born of God, we continue not in sin.

- **2 John 1:**
  - **Before You Read:** John's Second Epistle is written from John to an unnamed "elect lady". Look for more themes of love and warnings of deception in this chapter.
  - **What You'll Read About:** John sends love to this elect lady and rejoices that her children walk in the truth. He teaches that we must love one another and keep the commandments, and not be deceived by those who say Christ has not come in the flesh. Do not support those who teach this false doctrine.

- **3 John 1:**
  - **Before You Read:** John's Third Epistle is addressed to Gaius, someone who is righteous in the face of opposition. "The elder" is the way John refers to himself in this epistle.
  - **What You'll Read About:** John expresses his joy in the faithfulness of Gaius, and his charity. He says another church leader, Diotrephes, is prideful and will not receive John. John writes that the people who do good are of God, and tells Gaius he will visit him shortly.

- **Jude:**
  - **Before You Read:** This epistle is written by Jude, brother to James and half-brother to Jesus Christ. In it, Jude writes to address a problem in the church of Christians embracing Pagan worship practices and thinking they were above the moral law. Look for JST in the footnotes.
  - **What You'll Read About:** Jude opens his epistle and teaches that we should earnestly contend for our faith. The Lord will destroy those who go against His commands, and Jude gives examples of angels who didn't keep their first estate (chose Lucifer's plan) and Sodom and Gomorrah. Jude points to a prophecy from Enoch about Christ's Second Coming and the judgment that He will bring. In the last days, people will be mockers who separate themselves from the Spirit. Jude counsels us to build ourselves up in the faith and abide in God's love and mercy.

SPIRITUAL GUIDING QUESTIONS

Question: What does it mean to you that God is light? How has He brought light into your life? (1 John 1:5)

Question: What are some ways you have built your relationship with God? How could you get to know God even better? (1 John 2:3)

Question: How do you avoid "loving" things in the world more than things that will exist forever? Why is this important to you? (1 John 2:15)

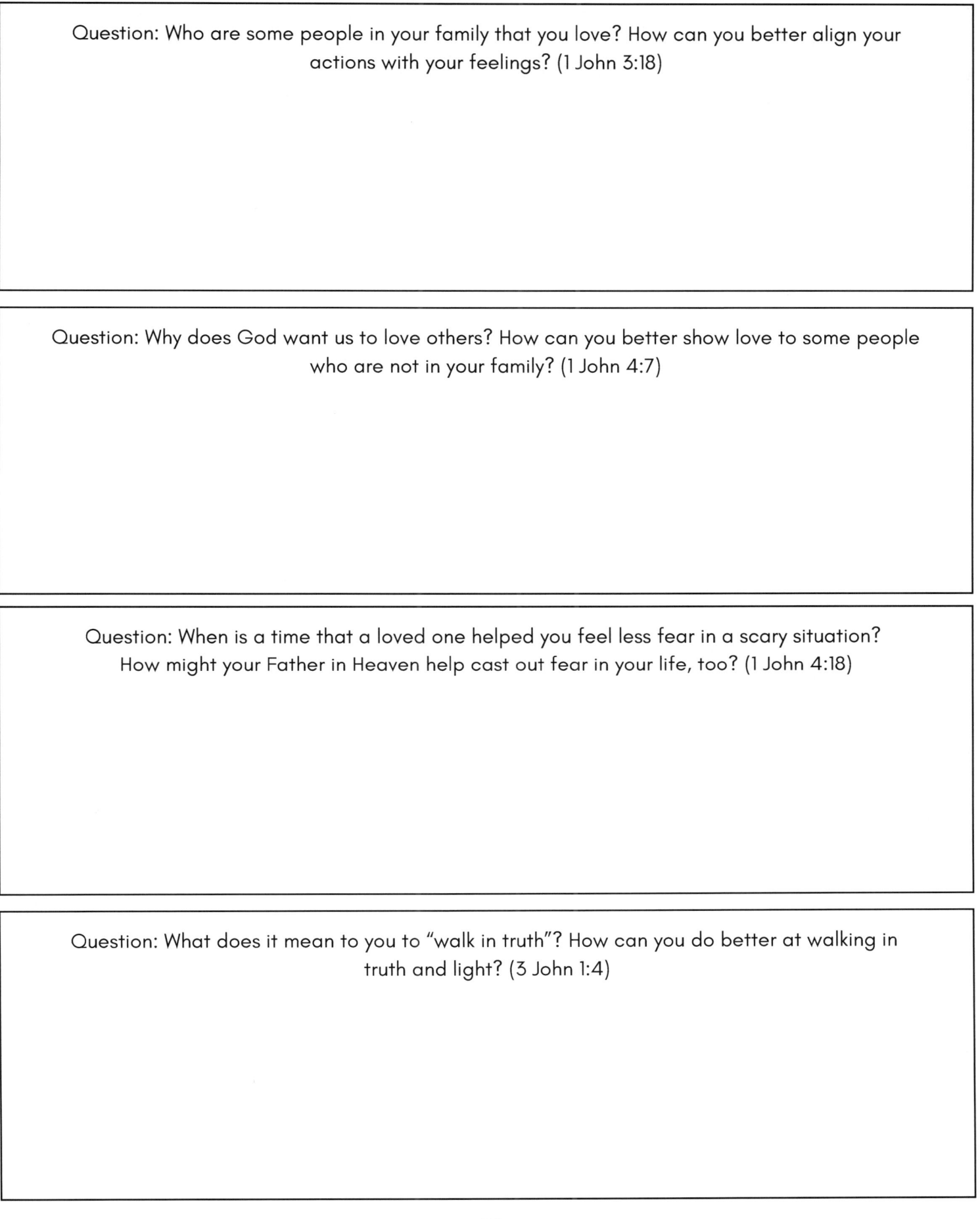

Question: Who are some people in your family that you love? How can you better align your actions with your feelings? (1 John 3:18)

Question: Why does God want us to love others? How can you better show love to some people who are not in your family? (1 John 4:7)

Question: When is a time that a loved one helped you feel less fear in a scary situation? How might your Father in Heaven help cast out fear in your life, too? (1 John 4:18)

Question: What does it mean to you to "walk in truth"? How can you do better at walking in truth and light? (3 John 1:4)

DECEMBER 4 - 10

REVELATION 1-5

"Glory, and Power, Be unto... the Lamb for Ever"

BIG PICTURE

How to feel confident fitting in this week's readings with the entire New Testament

General Context:

- **We begin the final book AND final section of the entire New Testament today!** You'll remember that the New Testament naturally splits into 4 categories: the four Gospels (Matthew-John); the missionary journeys (Acts); the epistles (Romans-Jude); and the revelation of the future (Revelation). The book of Revelation, split into 22 chapters, completes our study of the New Testament by looking to the future.
- **Who wrote the Revelation?** This revelation was recorded by John, apostle to Jesus and leader in the early Christian church that was quickly approaching apostasy. At the time, he was banished to the island of Patmos, a small island off the coast of modern-day Turkey. It was near the town of Ephesus, where he had been staying and preaching for a while. On Patmos, John had a vision outlining some of the most important events of the coming millennia. In it, Jesus Christ Himself instructed John to record what he was seeing, which he did in a book that is now called Revelation. It is difficult to know when John wrote this, although he likely had good knowledge of what the wicked Emperor Nero was doing to believers. This means the revelation was recorded as early as A.D. 68, but could have been later, around A.D. 90.
- **Revelation can be split into 2 parts: Chapters 1-3** cover current events that John and other saints were dealing with at the time. John was being given a heavenly perspective on what the church was facing in various cities. **Chapters 4-22** turn John toward future events. So this week, we will study contemporary events for John, and start just a little bit on future revelations.
- **Up until about the 14th century, Revelation was actually called Apocalypse.** "Apocalypse" comes from Greek and Latin roots meaning "to uncover or reveal" something, referring to this revelation revealing the ultimate fate of the world. Today, apocalypse refers to a destructive and cataclysmic event, which stems from this book that describes destruction and the end of the world.

- **Don't put too much pressure on yourself while reading this book!** The Book of Revelation can be one of those books of scripture that is quite daunting due to its extended symbolism. There are certain symbols that you will want to know, but it may not be possible to understand every single reference John makes. After all - he was having a heavenly vision and was experiencing some things that may have been impossible to describe! Try to focus on getting general themes, such as the eventual triumph of good over evil and the glorious ending that awaits the faithful. Understanding the symbols only helps if it leads us to these bigger spiritual themes.
- **One cool doctrine revealed in this week's reading has to do with whether or not animals will be resurrected!** In Revelation 5:11-14, we'll read about animals being resurrected and enduring in heaven forever. Joseph Smith even clarified, as recorded in D&C 77:3, that animals will be resurrected and found in heaven.

Spiritual Themes:

Look for these themes as you read the chapters this week! Find examples in the scriptures, and ponder on what these themes can look like in your life.

- **Worship Jesus Christ**

- **Overcome the World**

- **Walk With God**

People to Know:

- **John**
  - John was one of Christ's original apostles. John was among the few who knew Jesus the best, along with Peter and John's brother James. They were the only 3 who saw Jesus raise Jairus' daughter from the dead and the only ones who were on the Mount of Transfiguration with Jesus. He had been a fisherman by trade and the Savior referred to John and his brother James as the "sons of thunder". After Christ's death, John ministered with Peter and spent a lot of time in Ephesus. He was eventually exiled to the island Patmos, which is where he received the vision contained in Revelation. Many other Christians believe that John is likely the only of the original apostles who died of old age (as opposed to martyrdom). However, revelation in both the Book of Mormon and the Doctrine and Covenants clarify that John has been allowed to remain on the earth as a ministering servant. (Check out 3 Nephi 28:6 and D&C 7 for more info on that!)

this week: where are we?

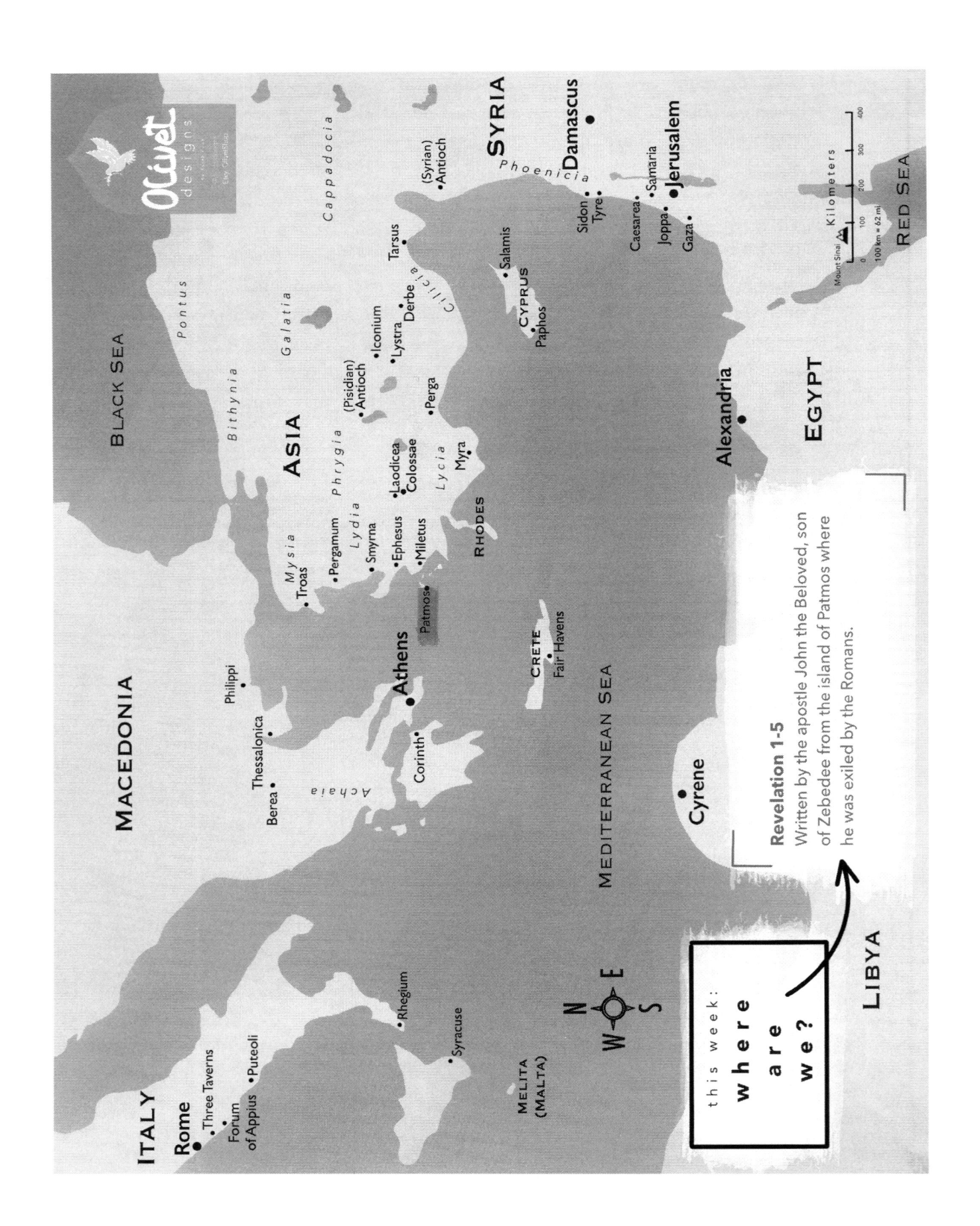

Revelation 1-5
Written by the apostle John the Beloved, son of Zebedee from the island of Patmos where he was exiled by the Romans.

LITTLE PICTURE
How to understand each chapter and apply principles to my life

- **Revelation 1:**
  - **Before You Read:** The apostle John is writing this Revelation following a vision he had of Jesus Christ. This first chapter serves as a sort of introduction, setting the scene for how and when he received this revelation. Look for JST in both the footnotes and the Appendix.
  - **What You'll Read About:** John describes a vision he received from Jesus Christ while on the island of Patmos. Christ will make us kings and priests, and will come again in glory in the clouds. John describes seeing Jesus among seven candlesticks. John falls down as if he were dead, and Christ tells him to fear not. Christ instructs John to write down this vision, and explains the meaning of the seven candlesticks.

- **Revelation 2:**
  - **Before You Read:** In the previous chapter, John explained how Christ appeared to him while on the island of Patmos and instructed him to write down the revelation he received. Look for JST in the footnotes.
  - **What You'll Read About:** Christ gives messages for John to send to each of four churches. To Ephesus, Jesus praises their works, patience, and the way they have rejected false apostles and secret combinations. He calls them to repent and return to their first love and good works. To Smyrna, Christ sends words of comfort and support that they will ultimately prevail if they are called to suffer and even die in this life. To Pergamos, Christ calls them to condemn idol worship and the meat sacrificed to idols. To Thyatira, Jesus calls them to repent for allowing a woman named Jezebel to sin. If we hold on and endure to the end, we can receive power and glory.

- **Revelation 3:**
  - **Before You Read:** In the previous chapter, John recorded messages Christ gave to four churches, which both praised them and called them each to repent in different ways. In this chapter, Christ will continue with messages to three more churches. Look for JST in the footnotes.
  - **What You'll Read About:** To Sardis, Christ instructs John to write that they must be watchful, because there are only a few in the city still worthy to walk with Christ. To Philadelphia, He praises those who have been patient and faithful, and gives them glorious promises. To the Laodiceans, Christ criticizes them for being "lukewarm" and loving riches. He chastens those He loves.

- **Revelation 4:**
  - **Before You Read:** Up until now, John has given some context on how he received this revelation, and then has written specific messages Christ gave to seven churches. Starting in chapter 4, he will start describing this vision he saw of the history and future of the world. If you want a little more information about some of the symbols in this chapter, Joseph Smith actually asked God about some of them, which you can read in D&C 77:1-5.
  - **What You'll Read About:** John is caught up in the spirit and sees the throne of God, with 24 elders dressed in white. He sees a sea of glass (the earth in its celestial state, see D&C 77:1) and four beasts full of eyes. The beasts, which can represent all creatures on earth, praise and worship the Lord.

- **Revelation 5:**
  - **Before You Read:** In the previous chapter, John described seeing the exalted earth and all living creatures worshiping at God's throne. Note the JST in verse 6, clarifying the symbolism in Christ's horns and eyes, and see D&C 77:6-7 for Joseph Smith's questions and answers concerning the seals on the book John sees.
  - **What You'll Read About:** John sees a book sealed with seven seals that no one is worthy to open. The Lamb of God comes forth, and the elders and beasts worship and praise Him. Thousands of thousands of angels join in, singing that the Lamb is worthy.

SPIRITUAL GUIDING QUESTIONS

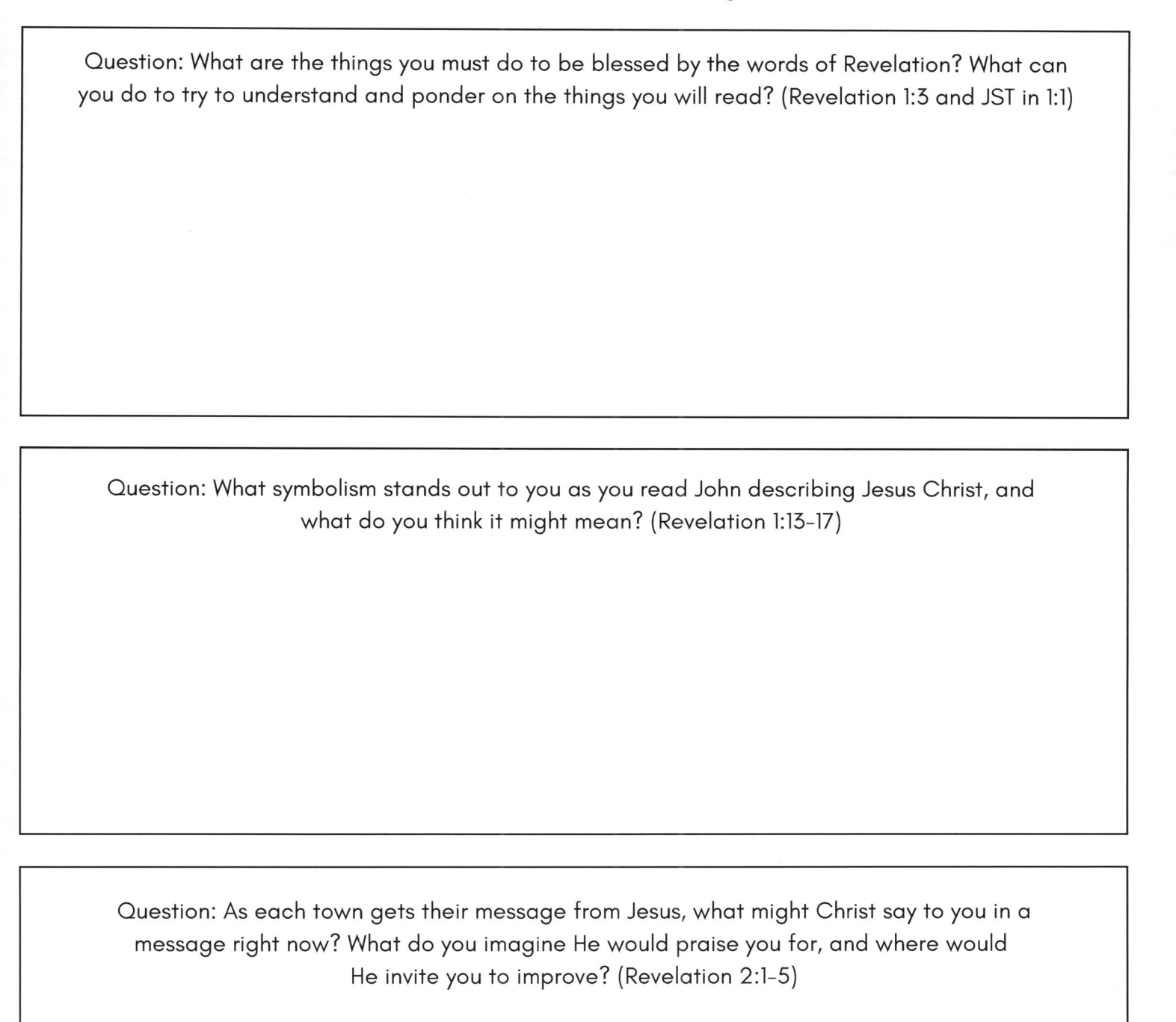

Question: What are the things you must do to be blessed by the words of Revelation? What can you do to try to understand and ponder on the things you will read? (Revelation 1:3 and JST in 1:1)

Question: What symbolism stands out to you as you read John describing Jesus Christ, and what do you think it might mean? (Revelation 1:13-17)

Question: As each town gets their message from Jesus, what might Christ say to you in a message right now? What do you imagine He would praise you for, and where would He invite you to improve? (Revelation 2:1-5)

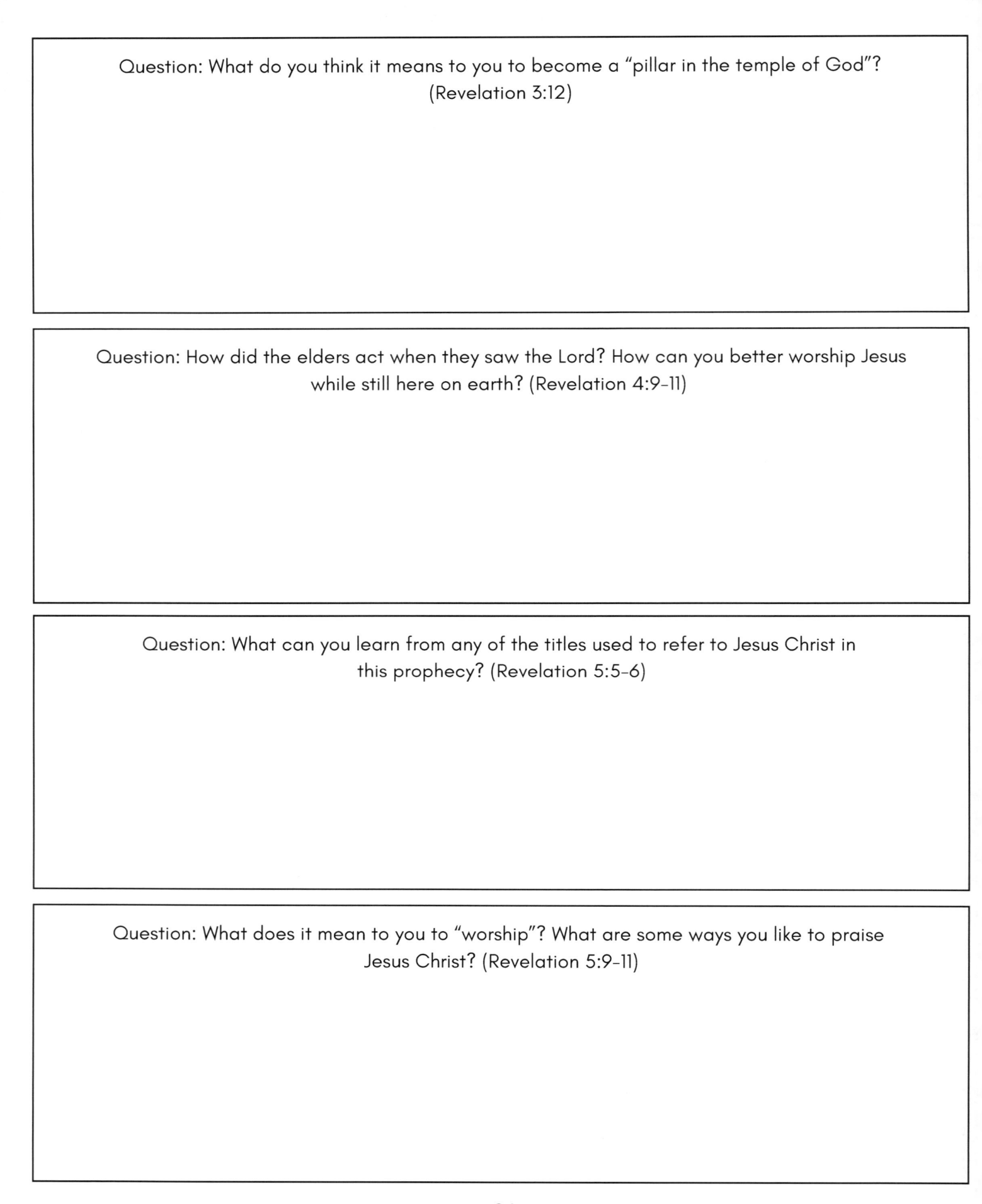

Question: What do you think it means to you to become a "pillar in the temple of God"? (Revelation 3:12)

Question: How did the elders act when they saw the Lord? How can you better worship Jesus while still here on earth? (Revelation 4:9-11)

Question: What can you learn from any of the titles used to refer to Jesus Christ in this prophecy? (Revelation 5:5-6)

Question: What does it mean to you to "worship"? What are some ways you like to praise Jesus Christ? (Revelation 5:9-11)

DECEMBER 11 - 17

REVELATION 6 - 14

"They Overcame... by the Blood of the Lamb"

BIG PICTURE

How to feel confident fitting in this week's readings with the entire New Testament

General Context:

- **Believe it or not, Joseph Smith said that Revelation was "one of the plainest books God ever caused to be written".** Getting bogged down in the symbolism of each verse can be a lengthy pursuit, but it seems like Joseph Smith understood that John's Revelation was best understood by zooming out to look at the big themes of good conquering evil, and Jesus' ultimate triumph.
- **As a quick context review, Revelation was written by the apostle John (yes, THAT John) on the island of Patmos.** John was living in exile there, and received this large vision that the Lord Himself commanded John to record. For the most part, John's Revelation deals with visions of what will happen in the future, including both the 2,000 years that have happened since John wrote this down and events that are still to come for us!
- **Did you know that Nephi saw John receiving this revelation?** When Nephi himself was caught up in his vision that took him through the history of the world as well as an explanation of the Tree of Life vision his father had, he specifically mentioned John. As Latter-day Saints, this further emphasizes that John's Revelation was a pivotal event and contains doctrines we need to study! Check out 1 Nephi 14:18-27 for all the details of Nephi's experience.
- **One unique prophecy contained in these chapters is found in the beginning of chapter 11.** This is where John describes that two prophets will lie dead in the streets of Jerusalem in the Last Days. The prophets will then be raised from the dead.

Spiritual Themes:

Look for these themes as you read the chapters this week! Find examples in the scriptures, and ponder on what these themes can look like in your life.

- **Being Cleansed by Jesus**

- **The Reality of the Adversary**

- **Preaching the Gospel**

People to Know:

- **John**
    - John was one of Christ's original apostles. John was among the few who knew Jesus the best, along with Peter and John's brother James. They were the only 3 who saw Jesus raise Jairus' daughter from the dead and the only ones who were on the Mount of Transfiguration with Jesus. He had been a fisherman by trade and the Savior referred to John and his brother James as the "sons of thunder". After Christ's death, John ministered with Peter and spent a lot of time in Ephesus. He was eventually exiled to the island Patmos, which is where he received the vision contained in Revelation. Many other Christians believe that John is likely the only of the original apostles who died of old age (as opposed to martyrdom). However, revelation in both the Book of Mormon and the Doctrine and Covenants clarify that John has been allowed to remain on the earth as a ministering servant. (Check out 3 Nephi 28:6 and D&C 7 for more info on that!)

this week: where are we?

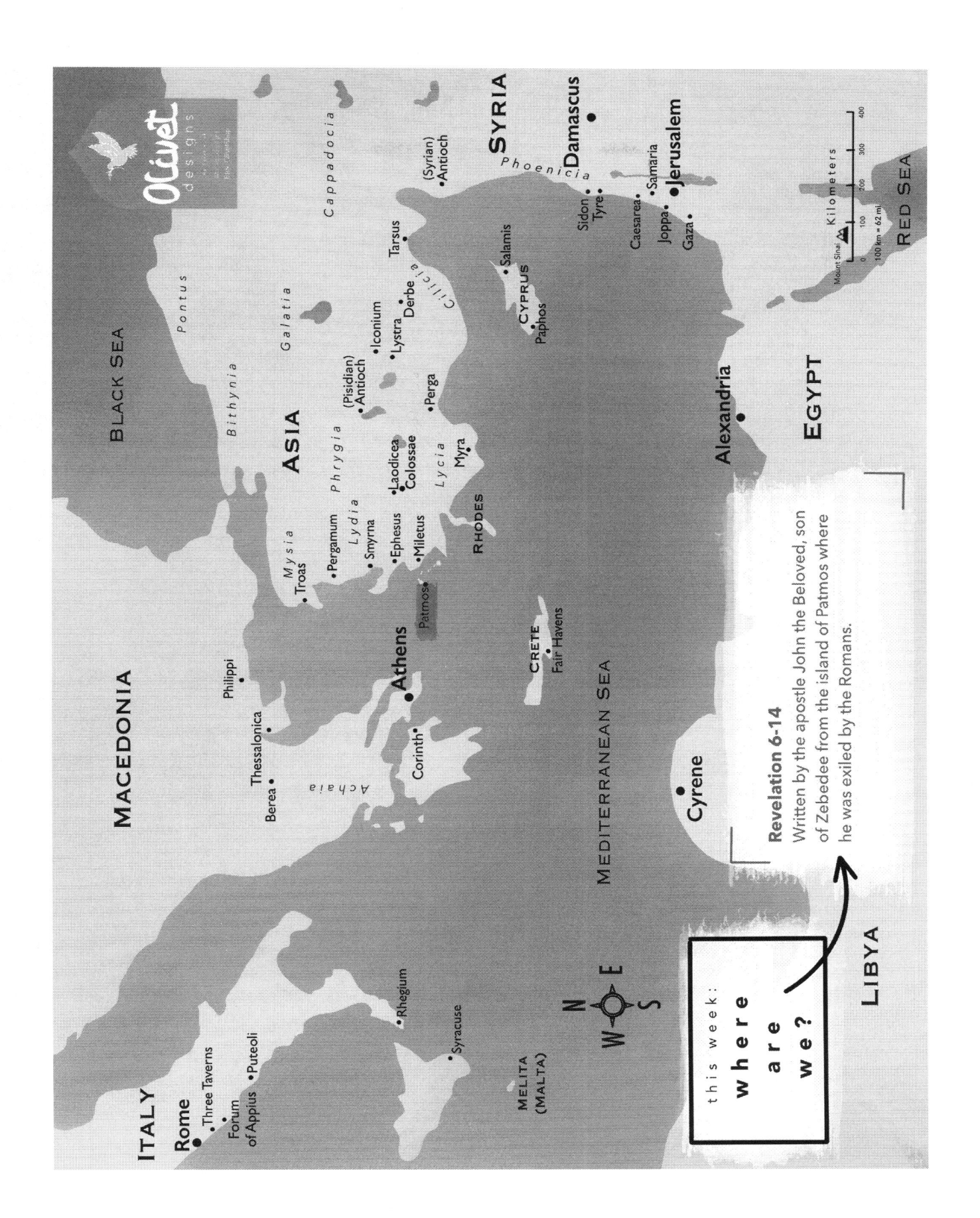

Revelation 6-14
Written by the apostle John the Beloved, son of Zebedee from the island of Patmos where he was exiled by the Romans.

LITTLE PICTURE
How to understand each chapter and apply principles to my life

- **Revelation 6:**
  - **Before You Read:** In the previous chapter, we were introduced to a book with 7 seals. We learn in D&C 77:7 that each seal represents one thousand years in the history of the earth. In this chapter, Christ opens the first six seals, which represent the first 6 millennia. Look for JST in the footnotes.
  - **What You'll Read About:** Christ is able to open the seals on the book we were introduced to in chapter 5. As each seal is opened, a beast asks John to come and see, and he sees a vision representing things happening in that period of one thousand years. He witnesses wars, famine, and destruction. As the fifth seal is opened, he sees Christians and apostles persecuted for their faith. When the sixth seal is opened, John witnesses great destruction and people hiding from disasters.

- **Revelation 7:**
  - **Before You Read:** In the previous chapter, Christ opened the first six seals of the sealed book, which represent the first six thousand years of this earth. A few of the symbols in this coming chapter, all in the first four verses, are ones Joseph Smith asked about in D&C 77:8-11.
  - **What You'll Read About:** John continues to describe what he saw upon the opening of the sixth seal. He describes angels, and 144,000 priests being sealed in their foreheads. John saw a great multitude of all kinds of people gathered before the throne of God with white robes, washed clean through the blood of Christ. The multitude serves God in the temple and Jesus makes sure their needs are met.

- **Revelation 8:**
  - **Before You Read:** In the previous chapter, John described what he saw when the sixth seal was opened, including a great multitude gathered who had been cleansed by Christ's blood. Note that Joseph Smith asks about the meaning of the trumpets mentioned in verse two of this chapter in D&C 77:12.
  - **What You'll Read About:** When the seventh seal is opened, there is silence followed by seven trumpets. Incense and the prayers of the saints ascend to God. As each of the first four angels sound their trumpets, there is destruction on the earth, destroying one third of trees, plants, sea creatures, and ships.

- **Revelation 9:**
  - **Before You Read:** John has been describing the events of the seventh seal. So far, four of the seven angels have sounded their trumpets, resulting in great destruction on earth. Look for JST in the footnotes.
  - **What You'll Read About:** The fifth angel sounds the trumpet, releasing scorpions and locusts to torment all except the men with the seal on the forehead for five months. The sixth angel releases four angels who cause wars that kill a third of the men. Men who remain after these plagues and wars continue to sin and worship other gods.

- **Revelation 10:**
  - **Before You Read:** In the previous chapter, John recounted more of the death and destruction he witnessed from the opening of the sixth seal. Remember each seal represents a thousand years of human history.
  - **What You'll Read About:** John describes more events from the sixth seal, which represents the last days before Christ's second coming. The seventh angel comes from heaven with might and thunder, landing on both the earth and sea. He gives John a book to eat, which represents John accepting his calling to gather the tribes of Israel.

- **Revelation 11:**
  - **Before You Read:** John has been describing his vision showing him the sixth seal, representing the last days before Christ's second coming.
  - **What You'll Read About:** John describes two witnesses who will prophesy with the power and protection of God in Jerusalem for three and a half years. They will then be killed and their bodies will lie in the street for three and a half days before being resurrected. There will be great destruction in Jerusalem when the prophets rise, and the elders gathered around God's throne will worship God. Nations will fear God's judgment.

- **Revelation 12:**
  - **Before You Read:** In the previous chapter, John told about the two prophets who will be killed in Jerusalem, then resurrected before the Second Coming. This entire chapter has a JST in the Appendix, which switches the order of some of the verses.
  - **What You'll Read About:** John sees a woman (often recognized as the church) who gives birth to a boy (often recognized as the kingdom of God). He also sees a great red dragon that represents Satan. There was a great war in heaven between the dragon and Michael's army of angels. The dragon lost and was cast out of heaven with his angels. The dragon then goes after the woman, but she is able to escape to the wilderness. The dragon decides to war against her posterity.

- **Revelation 13:**
  - **Before You Read:** In the previous chapter, John began a description of a war in heaven with a dragon (Satan) and Michael, which resulted in the dragon being cast down to earth where he tried to attack the kingdom of God on earth. Look for JST in the footnotes.
  - **What You'll Read About:** John sees a beast with great power that gets its strength from the dragon. The wicked people worship the beast and the dragon because of their great power. The beast fights and has power over the saints of God for some time. A second beast arises that looks like a lamb, but speaks like a dragon. John describes the power and abilities of this beast and those who follow it.

- **Revelation 14:**
  - **Before You Read:** John has been telling about the beasts that get their power from Satan, and how they will have power over the earth for a time.
  - **What You'll Read About:** The Lamb will stand on Mount Zion with 144,000 saints who have been redeemed. John sees an angel flying from heaven with the everlasting gospel to preach to all nations. Two more angels declare that Babylon has fallen, and condemn anyone who worships the beast. Blessed are those who die in the Lord. John sees angels with sickles ready to harvest the wicked and cast them into a winepress.

SPIRITUAL GUIDING QUESTIONS

Question: What could be the significance of the symbol John uses of God sealing us on the forehead? Why do you think he chose the forehead? (Revelation 7:2-3)

Question: What do we learn about those in the Celestial Kingdom? (Revelation 7:9)

Question: How is prayer like the smoke of incense? What is one way you could improve your prayers? (Revelation 8:3)

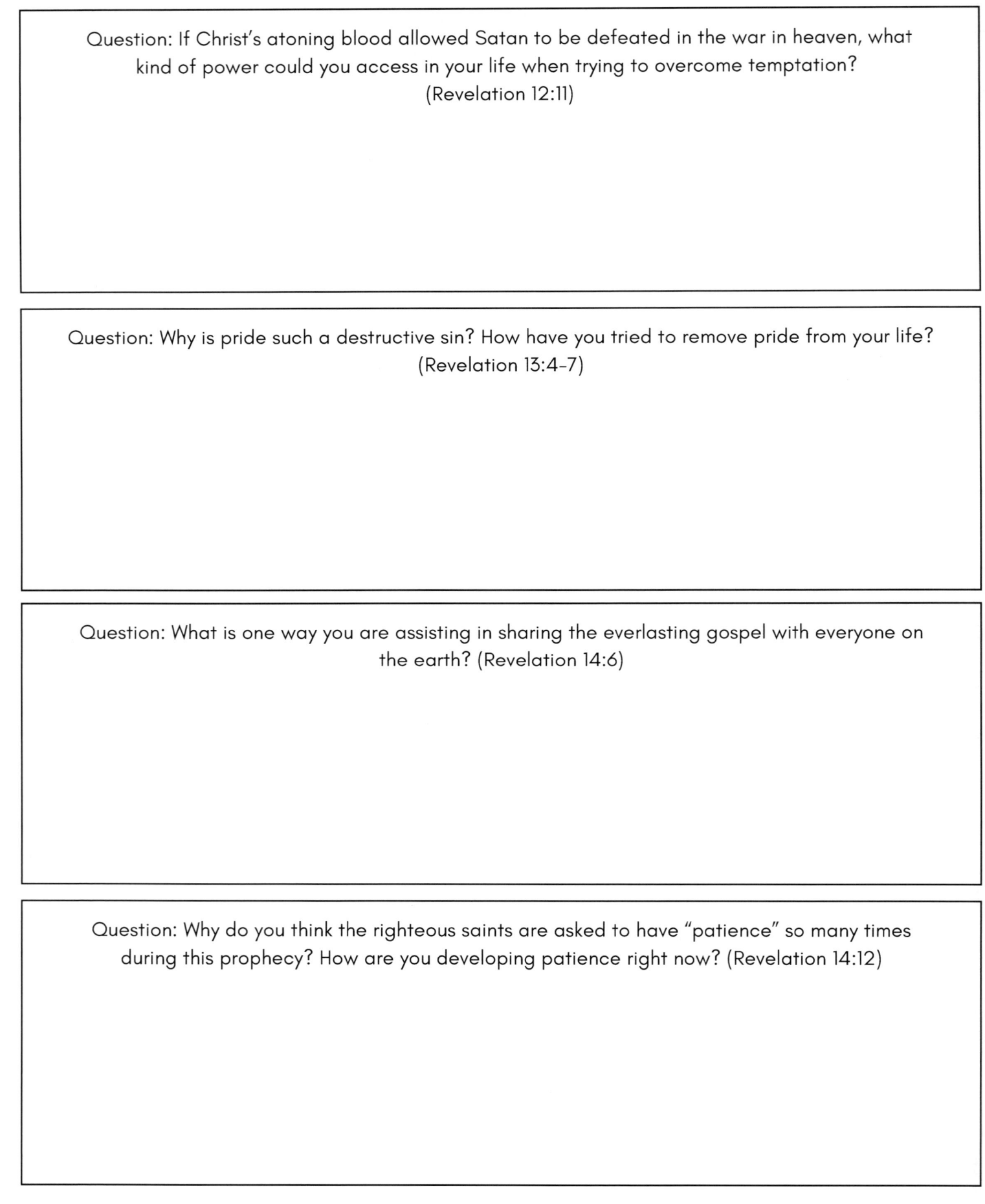

Question: If Christ's atoning blood allowed Satan to be defeated in the war in heaven, what kind of power could you access in your life when trying to overcome temptation? (Revelation 12:11)

Question: Why is pride such a destructive sin? How have you tried to remove pride from your life? (Revelation 13:4-7)

Question: What is one way you are assisting in sharing the everlasting gospel with everyone on the earth? (Revelation 14:6)

Question: Why do you think the righteous saints are asked to have "patience" so many times during this prophecy? How are you developing patience right now? (Revelation 14:12)

DECEMBER 25 - 31

REVELATION 15 - 22
"He That Overcometh Shall Inherit All Things"

BIG PICTURE
How to feel confident fitting in this week's readings with the entire New Testament

General Context:

- **Have you noticed that John wasn't the only one to receive a "guided tour" revelation from an angel?** John didn't just have various images brought to his mind as part of a large revelation - there was an angel guiding him through what he was seeing, and explaining certain elements. This seems to be a pattern in other revelations we can read about from other prophets, including Nephi, Ezekiel, Daniel, and Enoch.

- **As a quick context review, the apostle John is the one who recorded the book of Revelation.** After spending his time with Jesus during all of His mortal ministry, we don't have too much information about what John was up to following Christ's resurrection. We know John spent some time in Jerusalem, and eventually made his way to Ephesus. We have three epistles from John, and we know he also wrote his Gospel account of Christ's life. At this point, John was banished to the island of Patmos. He received this Revelation and was commanded to write it down.

- **The Apostasy and Restoration are over now, right?** Two topics that John's Revelation continues to discuss are the Apostasy of the gospel and the Restoration of the gospel, both of which had not happened yet in John's time. But if there's anything that modern revelation has taught us, it's that the Restoration is a continual event. It started with Joseph Smith, but new truths, principles, and higher ways of living will continue to be restored to the earth. On a personal level, we each need to also have gospel truths restored and accepted into our hearts. In the same sense, the Apostasy is not completely over. Apostasy, or the absence of priesthood power and covenants, still cover many areas, and can absolutely be found on a personal level, too.

- **So what happened to John?** As we finish up the entire New Testament, we don't get closure on many of the individuals we have read about within the actual scriptural texts that we have. We have to rely on tradition or other documents from that time period to get a glimpse into the brutal ending that each of the apostles, including Paul, endured as they were martyred for their beliefs. John, however, has a unique ending! While many other Christians believe that John must have been the only apostle to die from old age, modern revelation has clarified that John has been allowed to remain on the earth as a ministering servant. He also helped to restore the Melchizedek priesthood to the earth around 1830 to Joseph Smith and Oliver Cowdery. Check out 3 Nephi 28:6 and D&C 7 for more details.

Spiritual Themes:

Look for these themes as you read the chapters this week! Find examples in the scriptures, and ponder on what these themes can look like in your life.

- **The Power of Covenants**

- **Destruction of the Wicked**

- **Living in the Presence of God and Jesus**

People to Know:

- **John**
    - John was one of Christ's original apostles. John was among the few who knew Jesus the best, along with Peter and John's brother James. They were the only 3 who saw Jesus raise Jairus' daughter from the dead and the only ones who were on the Mount of Transfiguration with Jesus. He had been a fisherman by trade and the Savior referred to John and his brother James as the "sons of thunder". After Christ's death, John ministered with Peter and spent a lot of time in Ephesus. He was eventually exiled to the island Patmos, which is where he received the vision contained in Revelation. Many other Christians believe that John is likely the only of the original apostles who died of old age (as opposed to martyrdom). However, revelation in both the Book of Mormon and the Doctrine and Covenants clarify that John has been allowed to remain on the earth as a ministering servant. (Check out 3 Nephi 28:6 and D&C 7 for more info on that!)

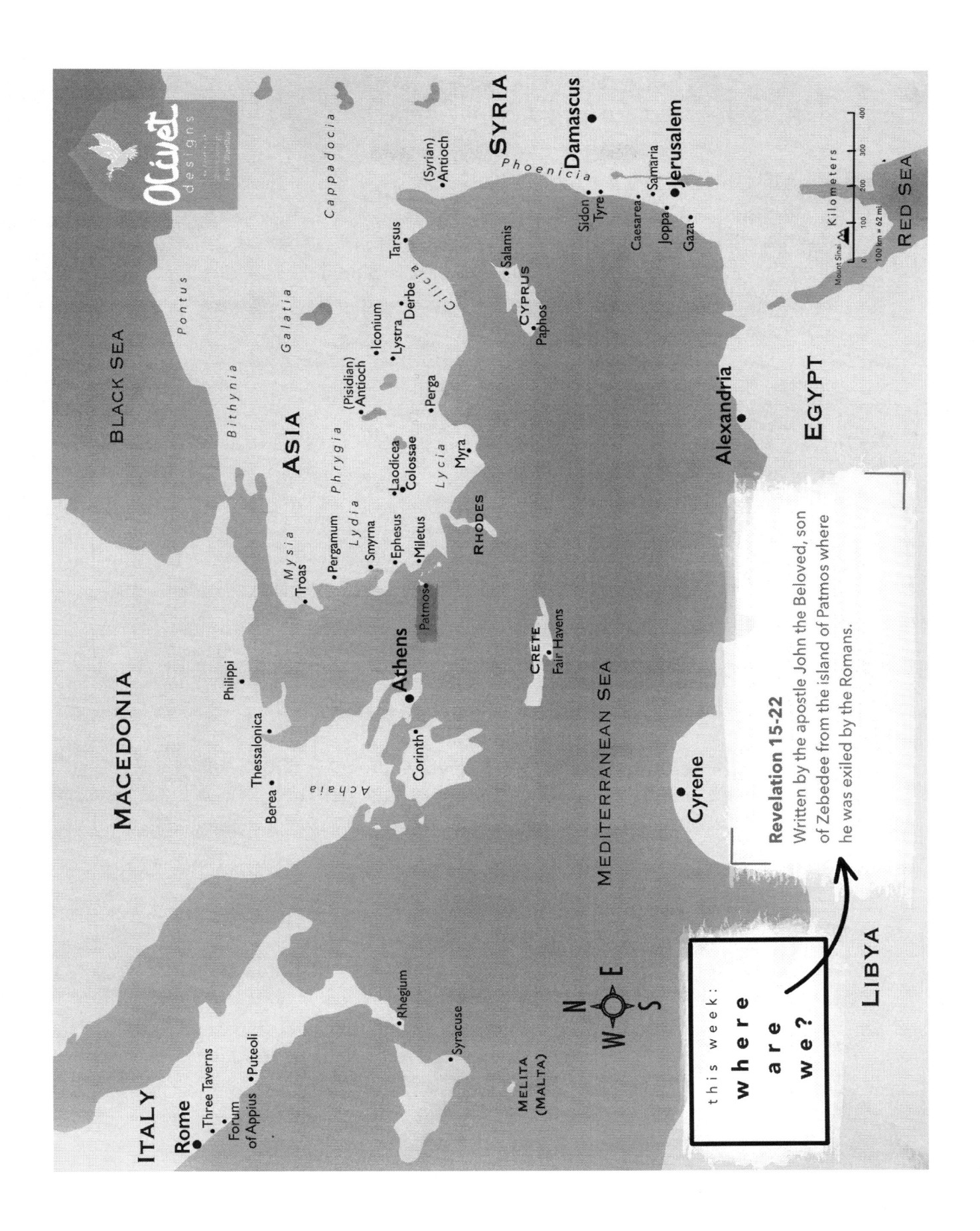

Revelation 15-22
Written by the apostle John the Beloved, son of Zebedee from the island of Patmos where he was exiled by the Romans.

this week: **where are we?**

LITTLE PICTURE
How to understand each chapter and apply principles to my life

- **Revelation 15:**
    - **Before You Read:** John has been writing about the last days, which he witnessed when the sixth seal was opened. He just described Jesus Christ harvesting the earth.
    - **What You'll Read About:** John describes a scene where those who triumphed over the beast sing and praise God on a sea of glass (exalted earth). Seven angels prepare to unleash plagues upon the wicked.

- **Revelation 16:**
    - **Before You Read:** In the previous chapter, John described seven angels getting ready to pour out plagues on the world.
    - **What You'll Read About:** John writes about the plagues that the seven angels bring in the last days, including turning water to blood and letting the sun scorch men with fire. Christ will come again as a thief, and people will be gathered to a place called Armageddon. John witnessed lightning, earthquakes, and hail on the earth.

- **Revelation 17:**
    - **Before You Read:** In the previous chapter, John saw plagues poured out on the earth and great destruction. The wicked did not repent.
    - **What You'll Read About:** John sees the great wickedness of Babylon, represented by a woman riding on a beast which comes from the bottomless pit. The wicked will fight against the Lamb and His followers. Followers of Satan, represented by the beast, will fight among themselves.

- **Revelation 18:**
    - **Before You Read:** In the previous chapter, John witnessed Satan's followers and Babylon gathering and fighting. The Lamb also gathered with His followers.
    - **What You'll Read About:** An angel comes from heaven to declare that Babylon has fallen, and to call the righteous from the city. God will judge Babylon and those with her for their riotous living. The wicked will mourn as Babylon burns and all her riches are wasted.

- **Revelation 19:**
    - **Before You Read:** In the previous chapter, Babylon fell and was destroyed quickly. Look for JST in the footnotes.
    - **What You'll Read About:** The righteous, including the 24 elders at God's throne, praise God and rejoice that the wicked are judged. The clean and righteous will be invited to the marriage supper of the Lamb. Jesus will come from heaven clothed in power and glory with His army. Christ will destroy the wicked with the sword and fire.

- **Revelation 20:**
    - **Before You Read:** John has described the destruction of Babylon and the wicked by Christ and His armies of the righteous. Look for JST in the footnotes.
    - **What You'll Read About:** John saw Satan bound for a thousand years, unable to deceive men. After the millennium, the dead will be resurrected and Satan will be loosed for a season to gather his soldiers to battle against the saints. God will devour the devil and his followers with fire. All will be judged out of the book of life, according to their works.

- **Revelation 21:**
    - **Before You Read:** In the previous chapter, John recounted his vision of Satan being bound for the millennium before all will be judged out of the book of life.
    - **What You'll Read About:** John describes the earth during the millennium, including the earth being renewed, Christ dwelling among men, and no death or sorrow. Those who overcome will be the children of God. Christ's bride is represented by the New Jerusalem. John describes the beauty of the new and exalted city of Jerusalem.

- **Revelation 22:**
    - **Before You Read:** In the previous chapter, John saw the glorious New Jerusalem descend from heaven during the Millennium. This is the final chapter in Revelation and the entire New Testament as a whole.
    - **What You'll Read About:** God's throne will sit beside a river of the water of life and the tree of life. An angel tells John that the things he saw are true, and that Christ will come quickly. The righteous will be in the celestial city with access to the tree of life and water of life. John teaches that we cannot change his words, and prays that Christ will come quickly.

SPIRITUAL GUIDING QUESTIONS

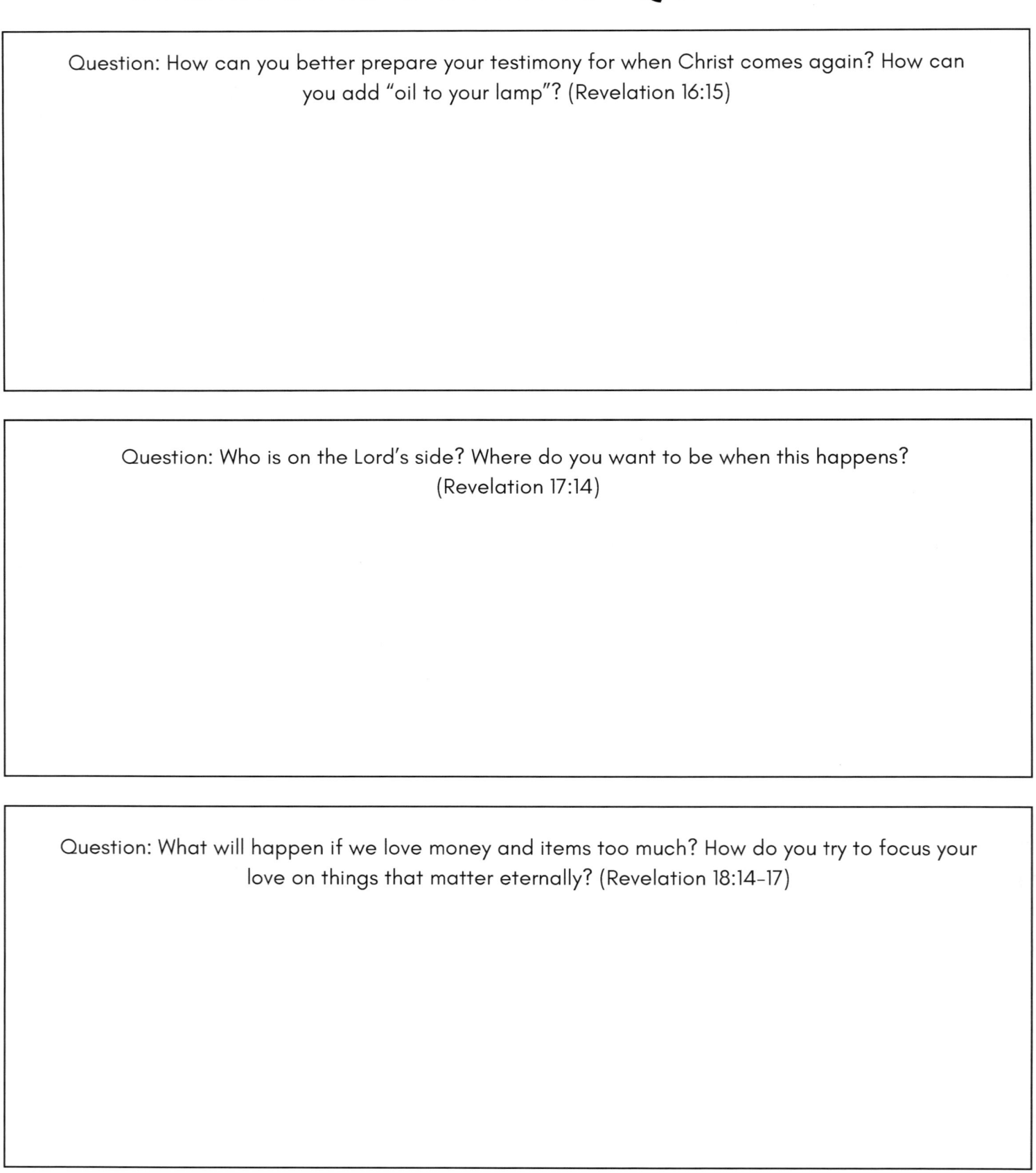

Question: How can you better prepare your testimony for when Christ comes again? How can you add "oil to your lamp"? (Revelation 16:15)

Question: Who is on the Lord's side? Where do you want to be when this happens? (Revelation 17:14)

Question: What will happen if we love money and items too much? How do you try to focus your love on things that matter eternally? (Revelation 18:14-17)

Question: What will life be like for the righteous while Satan is bound for 1,000 years? (Revelation 20:4)

Question: Although this is a slightly impossible question, what might it be like to dwell permanently in the presence of God and Jesus? What emotions might be present? (Revelation 21:3-4)

Question: Why is there no need for a temple in the New Jerusalem? What does that teach you about the importance of temples currently? (Revelation 21:22)

Question: How will Jesus be a light? In what ways is Jesus currently a light in your life? (Revelation 21:23)

Congratulations for finishing October-December in the New Testament!

Ready for more Come, Follow Me resources?

Check comefollowmestudy.com or my social media channels @comefollowmestudy for more information on how to get any New Testament study guides you may have missed, as well as information about the next study guides for the Book of Mormon! Thank you for your continued support.

Got any questions or feedback? I'd love to hear from you at comefollowmestudy@gmail.com.

Created by Cali Black, Come Follow Me Study, LLC. This material is copyrighted. It is intended for use in one household. For additional permissions, contact Cali at comefollowmestudy@gmail.com.

This material is neither made, provided, approved, nor endorsed by Intellectual Reserve, Inc. or The Church of Jesus Christ of Latter-day Saints. Any content or opinions expressed, implied or included in or with the material are solely those of the owner and not those of Intellectual Reserve, Inc. or The Church of Jesus Christ of Latter-day Saints.

Made in the USA
Columbia, SC
15 September 2023